HAVERA

the story of an island

HAVERA

the story of an island

To the Havera folk

J Laughton Johnston . Christine De Luca . Mark Sinclair . Pauleen Wiseman

Havera

First published in 2013 by Shetland Amenity Trust,
Garthspool, Lerwick, Shetland, ZE1 0NY

ISBN: 978−0−9572031−1−2

Designed & Produced by Millgaet Media
North Ness Business Park
Lerwick
Shetland
ZE1 OLZ

millgaet media

Preface

Havera is one of those small Shetland isles that has a special mystique. Like many, it was once inhabited but *it* has the singular honour of being one of the last to hold a community. It is a place that would be high on the list of any island lover as it has been on mine all my time in Shetland. I had often wondered when it was settled, who were the people of that community, how did they make a living and why did they leave?

In April 2011, I met Bobby Hunter on the North boat coming home from Aberdeen. At some point, the conversation turned to the island of (South) Havera. Bobby told me he was one of four co−owners and that they still kept sheep there. Then he began to tell me more; about shipwrecks, the wind mill, the story of the drowning of the laird, the fertility of the land and the bounty of the sea, the women sailing eight miles to Scalloway for their shopping and finally, when the families left Havera that they had bought the *Girl Lizzie*, a state of the art steam drifter. How did the families of a fishing and crofting community of an island less than a mile square find the wherewithal to buy such an expensive fishing boat?

I immediately wanted to write about it! But before I went any further I did some research in the Shetland Museum and Archives to see just what was available. It turned out that there was not a great deal of recorded history of Havera. However, there were three tapes made by two brothers and a sister who had all been born there in the first decades of the 20th century, just before everyone left. These tapes told a very human story of life on the island, the close cooperation and intimate society of four or five families living in a tight little township and their sadness in having to leave.

Although the history of Havera, prior to the community, is of great interest and played − for such a tiny island − an important part in Shetland's story, I have touched on it only lightly, as it is the human story of the community I wanted to tell.

But, apart from the written text, how can a writer capture the unique atmosphere of such a magical place as Havera and the character of its people? It seemed to me that prose, alone, and 'English' prose at that, would be inadequate. I could print the recordings of the last born there but that peculiarly Shetland aura created by the voices would be missing. I decided therefore that the book should make use of other creative media to supplement the text.

I therefore invited the poet Christine De Luca to participate in the book. After just one visit to Havera she produced several poems that captured just what I wanted. From that point on Christine became a co−editor, particularly keeping an eye on my use of Shetland dialect. We then approached the other three co−owners and with their support and assistance − without whom this book could not have been written − I patched together the story of Havera that still exists. Finally, we invited the Shetland photographer Mark Sinclair and musician Pauleen Wiseman to join us in both a book and DVD. They not only wholeheartedly participated, but their own unique contributions, along with that of Christine De Luca, are responsible for its final shape and structure; a far more fitting tribute to the people of Havera than I could have done alone.

The majority of the figures in the photographs have been identified but sadly there is not space to name them all, nor to include all the inhabitants on the family trees in the Appendix: only those mentioned in the text are included. All individuals mentioned in the text, where known, are given their birth date in brackets so that they may be identified, as many have both the same forename and surname.

This is not a definitive history of Havera but a portrait of the island and its people. In many ways it is representative of other − once inhabited − islands of Shetland; even Scotland: islands that will continue to lose their communities, their history, their stories.

Acknowledgements

This book could not have been written without the support and assistance of the owners and managers of (South) Havera: Adalene Fullerton, Bobby Hunter, Brenda Isbister, Robert Jamieson and Iris Jamieson, to whom I am very grateful. They supplied most of the stories and the old photographs of the Havera folk. I am grateful in addition to George Jamieson and Joann Balfour who also supplied photographs and the latter, Jessie's early reading book. In addition, the Shetland Museum and Archives supplied several photographs and facsimiles of documents for which I am grateful. Shetland Radio kindly gave permission to quote from recordings and the census is courtesy of Scotlandspeople.

I would especially like to thank Bobby Hunter for originally sparking my interest in Havera and for transporting myself, my collaborators and others, to and from Havera, on a number of occasions.

I would like to thank the poet Christine De Luca, photographer Mark Sinclair and musician Pauleen Wiseman whose contributions have made the book and the coming DVD so much richer and attractive. Although the original idea for the book was mine, its final form and appearance owes a great deal to them. I am particularly grateful to Christine De Luca who joined me in the project at its earliest stages and who became a co-editor and valued contributor and critic throughout its development.

I would like to thank the staff of the Shetland Museum and Archives and the Shetland Amenity Trust; particularly Blair Bruce, Eileen Brooke-Freeman, Trevor Jamieson, Angus Johnson, Emma Miller, Brian Smith, Ian Tait, Val Turner and Joanne Wishart, for answering my questions and for pointing me in the right direction on numerous occasions. Eileen Brooke-Freeman, with the help of the Burra History Group and others, also produced the Havera place-names map. I am grateful to Ron Jamieson and Sandra Pearson for permission to publish extracts from Andrew Jamieson's account of fishing from Havera in his youth. Several other people gave me their time and their recollections of Havera stories, including Robert Leask and George P S Peterson, to whom I am also grateful; the Havera rig-names are from the latter's hand-drawn map. My thanks also go to Richard Gibson who has drawn the first plan of the wind mill.

A vital part of the whole is the DVD, which is to be released later. I applaud the courage of Adalene Fullerton, Brenda Isbister and Bobby Hunter for agreeing to read the text. I would also like to thank Christine De Luca for reading her poems and Pauleen Wiseman for composing and playing her original Shetland airs that grace the spoken word. The various recordings were done at Mareel by Iain Waddell and Jonathan Rich who have made such a wonderful job of seamlessly weaving them together.

Lastly, I am grateful to Jimmy Moncrieff and the Shetland Amenity Trust for agreeing to publish the book; to Davy Cooper for the inset map on page 8, and for giving the project his enthusiastic support and guiding the book through the process of publication; also to Craig Sim of Millgaet for setting its many aspects – the text, poetry, extracts and photos – into the framework of the finished book.

Finally, the *Ann* – the Havera summer fishing boat 'launched' together with the book – was donated to the Shetland Museum and Archives by Iris and Brian Jamieson. There, it was skillfully and lovingly restored by Jack Duncan and Robbie Tait, with the ironwork carried out by Erik Erasmuson.

Havera

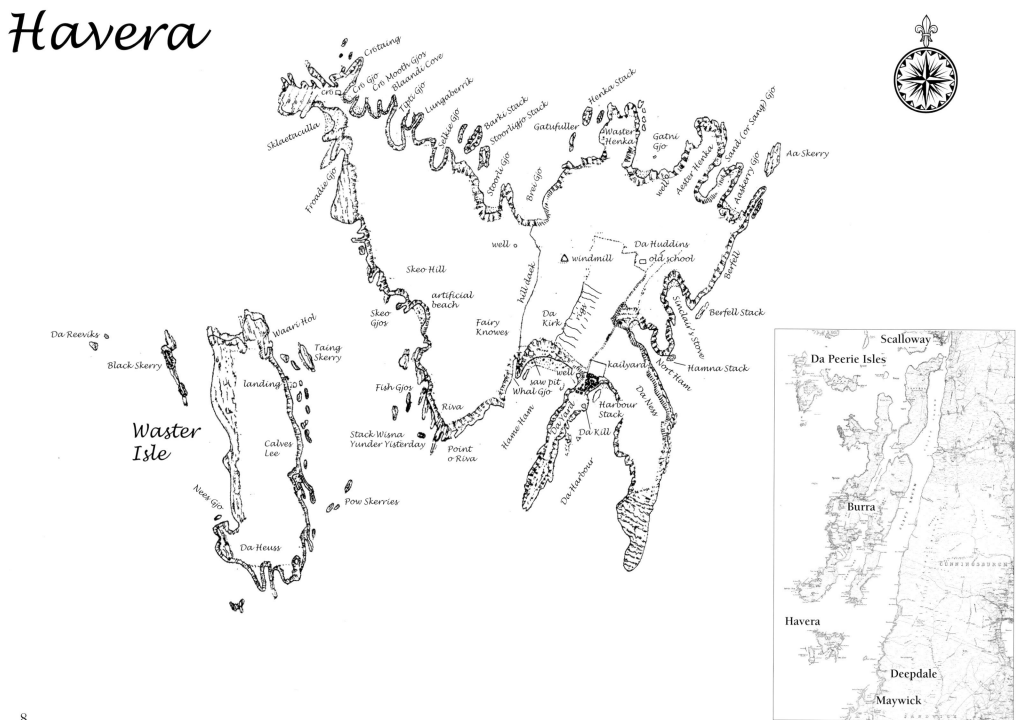

Crotaing
Cró Gjo
Cró Mooth Gjos
Blaandi Cove
Cró
Tipti Gjo
Lungaberrik
Selkie Gjo
Barki Stack
Stoorligjo Stack
Henka Stack
Gatufuller
Waster Henka
Gatni Gjo
Aester Henka
Sand (or Sang) Gjo
Aa Skerry
Aaskerry Gjo
well
Sklaetaculla
Froadie Gjo
Stoorli Gjo
Brei Gjo
well
Da Huddins
windmill
old school
Berfell
Skeo Hill
hill daek
Da Kirk
rigs
Sinclair's Stone
Berfell Stack
artificial beach
Da Reeviks
Skeo Gjos
Fairy Knowes
well
saw pit
Whal Gjo
kailyard
Nort Ham
Hamna Stack
Waari Hol
Taing Skerry
Black Skerry
landing
Fish Gjos
Da Yard
Da Kill
Da Ness
Waster Isle
Calves Lee
Riva
Stack Wisna Yunder Yisterday
Point o Riva
Hame Ham
Harbour Stack
Da Harbour
Nees Gjo
Pow Skerries
Da Heuss

Inset map

Scalloway
Da Peerie Isles
Burra
Havera
Deepdale
Maywick

Mappin Havera

Havera's aa namit fae da sea.
We could box da compass
o wir isle; hits names markin
ivery sklent da sea is med,
da taings an stacks an gyos.

If on your wye ta Havera
an mist rowled in,
ivery steekit bicht spelt danger;
you had ta ken dem, ivery een.

Comin fae Maywick
you can hardly miss Da Ness,
graet neb o laand, a faersome *point*.
Gie dat een a wide berth.

Roond tae da suddert
der Da Harbour – Göd kens
foo dat name cam ta be – wi waves
aff da Atlantic birsed in atween
twa fingers o laand, cloorin a cave
anunder banks. Keep clear.

You'll maybe scrime wir hooses
at Da Yard – *weel, we hed wir skroos dere,*
but maybe some aalder name
wis buckled up an changed?
You'd tink at sailors widda fun
a better name for hit.
Maybe hit wis cried 'De Ver'
da sea rock; da place whaar
birds bred or fysh spaaned.
Hit points sooth atween Da Harbour
an Haem Ham, nedder wan o dem
a *haven*; we hed ta laand *nort* by.

Whitivver, bide clean ootbye
da Point o Riva, dat *rocky cleft*, an Fysh Gyo;
weel aff da Waster Isle wi hits paand
o skerries. You'll maybe scrime
da peerie beach an örmals o da saat store at
Skeo Gyos – say hit fast – da Skyuggies.

Up bi wast, watch for waves brakkin
owre dat *baa*, Da Reeviks; *da lönabrak,*
da foamy styooch o Froadie Gyo.

Nor bi nor–wast der Crö Taing,
da point o laand whaar we caa'd da sheep;
dan roond nor–aest ta Crö Gyos
whaar we took dem aff.
Dat neuk is lik a haand rekkin oot
ta yokk a hadd o you. Bide weel awa.

Dan aa da treachery o boannie peerie gyos
aroond da nort end: Tipti – or mair lik Topti – Gyo
whaar dey man a bön a hoose,
an deeper Blaandi, da name missed oot
apö da map; *dey shurley couldna match*
da kirn-mylk colour tae da watter.
An Longaberrick – *heddery banks?*
Or whaar longies lodged an watcht
sels tirl in Selkie Gyo or dook dem
trowe da arch o Barki Stack.
Wis dat whaar aert-bark
bloomed hits tickest?

Maybe dey'll be shalter
ithin Stourli Gyo. I doot him.
Keep gyaain till you gyet your bearins,
an fin Brei Gyo, da *broad* een.

Bide affa Waster Henka,
whaar da trows danced,
an Gatufuller, whaar grice
roond Gatni Gyos *headicraad*
biblically owre da banks?
Keep gyaain, but watch
for a line o peerie stacks.
If you're won ta Saandy Gyo, keep affa
Aaskerry, dat *sindered promentary.*

Roond tae da aest der
Berfell, *steep rocky banks.*
Da Gyo ca'ad Sinclair's Stove luiks tizin,
but no; keep trivellin sooth.
Could dat be Sinclair's Stofa,
whaar da muckle hoose o Olaf Sinclair sat;
da laa man, Shetland's Foud?

Waves'll brack roond Hamna Stack
guardin da Nort Ham,
wir peerie *haven*.
Mak for dere if you can.

Contents

ONE

DA STERT

In 1911 the census for the island of South Havera (hereafter referred to simply as Havera), just south of Burra on the west coast of Shetland, indicated a healthy and sustainable population of 29 adults and children. The families had lived on this almost cliff–bound isle of considerably less than a square mile since their great great grandparents had been settled there as tenants some 150 years before. However, all was not well.

The island could only support a limited number of people. Young, growing families, particularly second or third sons or daughters who did not succeed to their parents' croft[i] and who had no means of livelihood had had to depart before. But when a stalwart of the island, David Williamson (1842) lost his wife in 1914, his eldest son and family having already departed in 1907 taking with them their household furnishings and all their belongings, he too left. There were now five remaining households. Six years later, in 1920, another son and family left, once more taking with them all their belongings and stock. The abandonment of Havera then accelerated. In 1921 David's nephew and family and another couple departed; then in 1922 James Jamieson (1847) departed when his wife died. That left just two households and *they* left in 1923. For the first time in many hundreds of years, perhaps even thousands, Havera was empty of human inhabitants. It was not only the end of an era for Havera, it was the end of an era for virtually all the very small isles of Shetland, for Havera was arguably the last to support a population. It is now 90 years since Havera was abandoned.

---

[i] Strictly speaking, the term 'croft' only became common usage later in the 19th century, but it is used here to describe the typical Shetland tenanted farm with its very limited area of *rigs* (arable ground) and shared grazings.

Havera folk c1916; James (Dey) Jamieson (1847) third from the left; David Williamson (1842) second from the right

"*Dey left becaas dey wir naeboady left ta geeng back an fore wi da boat … becaas da young men wis aa laevin … weel, dey wirna laevin exactly, dey wir aa gyaain tae da fishin … [so] dey wir straandit becaas da twa owld men wis turnt owre owld an dey wir comin ta eichty dan. So, dat wye dey wir naeboady ta steer dis boat, dis saily-boat, back an fore. So dey towt, an I believe dat, if dey hed lived anidder year in Havera, dey nivvir widda left. Dey aa said dat becaaas da motor boat cam eftir dat. An onyboady could a learned da motor boat. …*
Hit wisna a very göd feelin [leaving Havera] … *tinkin you wir laevin haem.*"
Jessie Goodlad (née Williamson 1903-2003)[1]

There are several written records of its history and, fortuitously, recordings were made in the 1970s and 1980s of three who were born there – Jessie (1903), John (1907) and Gideon Williamson (1912). This is the story of Havera and the families that lived there and of its last years told by these three old folk and from traditions handed down by word of mouth to the present descendants. A sister of those three, May Jane Ward (née Williamson 1914), is the last living person to be born on Havera. She was born the day one of the largest ships in the world, the *Oceanic*, ran onto a reef and sank at Foula, 25 miles (40 km) to the west, almost within sight of Havera. The story of the families is not only unique in that their community lived on such a tiny island and made such a success of it, but it is also representative of the daily struggle and the indispensable need for co–operation that made all Shetland's crofting and fishing communities of the 19th century sustainable, often barely so.

Not much more than one hundred years ago today, not only was every scrap of potentially arable land occupied on the mainland of Shetland, but many of the smallest islands – some barely half a square mile – were also home to crofting and fishing folk, eking out their precarious existence. The peak of occupation of these fragments of land was probably in the second half of the 19th century when Shetland's population was at its maximum and before emigration reached its peak; when landlords, with rough persuasion, continued to encourage new ground to be broken, new families of fishermen to be established, for the rent and income they would provide.

Access, size and soils were perhaps the key criteria for occupation of these islands. People had to be able to land a boat safely and keep it secure above high water, and there needed to be enough soil to provide the basic staples of potatoes, oats and bere and enough rough ground to support sheep and at

least one cow. Many of these islands supported but one extended family, others up to five or more. All had boats, of course, but for those relying almost entirely on the croft for subsistence, these simply provided transport to and from the mainland when needed and for the regular foray for fish to augment their limited fare. Only a few of the small islands, in Yell Sound and off Burra, exploited fishing as the principal income. But the Burra islands were exceptional, where good fishing – at the *haaf* – was closer inshore than anywhere else in Shetland.

Gradually, however, that island way of life became untenable, through the lack of able bodies as the young men and women left; the former – in the case of Havera – to fish from the new and larger decked fishing boats or to emigrate; and the latter to marry or find seasonal jobs in the herring industry. But also, as living standards rose, fewer and fewer people were prepared to live with the additional hardships that came with island life. The young, no

doubt, having got a taste of a wider society, became reluctant to return.

It has been suggested that the name Havera derives either from Old Norse (ON) *hafr*, meaning a man's name or a he–goat[2], or from *hafri*, meaning oats[3]. Of the three it is perhaps the last that rings true as the soils are so good and the most recent inhabitants often commented on the quality of their crops. The island is relatively isolated, just south of the much larger and well–populated islands of West and East Burra one mile (1.6 km) to the north and the Shetland mainland a little less than that to the east. Another six miles (10 km) or so to the north and offshore lie several islands of a similar size to Havera that shared its predominantly fishing economy. These are Hildasay, Papa, Langa, Linga and Oxna, affectionately known as the 'Peerie Isles'. They were the penultimate small isles to be inhabited by more than one family, their people remaining almost as long as those on Havera.

" … if we wir dön wi dellin first, or wan o da neebirs wis dön wi dellin first…bere wis da thing dat wis delled first … bere rigs … da fowr rigs tagidder… dan aa hed ta pit da sam i da rigs sae as iverythin was sware … an if we wir dön wi first, or if, say, Davie Williamson was dön wi first, dey didna kerry on wi da ots afore dey feenished aa wis aff. Dey wir a owld man an a owld wife at hed da laand an we aa gud an feenished dem aff … dey couldna manage ithoot dat. An dat's whit we did aa da time. We nivver tocht ta dö your ain an leave some idder boady i da lurch … Naeboady fell oot an naeboady ivver flet on een anidder."
Jessie

Namin da Peerie Isles

Fae da *Green Holm* scarfs arrow low
mallies bank stiffly troo sea furrows.

Papa, *priest isle*: der nane ta lay
haands on, ta sain noo.

Linga, *hedder isle*: a sea hairst –
piltocks, whelks, selkies, waar.

Hildis isle: tree score o sels neebin
slidder ta safety in Tangi Voe.

Da Shingies: *rocks in sun* at spills gowld.
Tirricks faest, dive low an wild.

Da sels is gien ta Hildasay daday.
Oksna: silent *seal isle*.

Pauleen Wiseman

The Peerie Isles are granite but the rocks of Havera have some gneiss and crystalline limestone that impart a fertility to the soil that is not present on the former or in many parts of Shetland.

Even in 1654 a visitor, Hugh Leigh, commented on this: *'It is all covered with grass. Here one Ew[e] hath very ordinarily two Lambs,'* adding … *'And here do no Mouse or Rat live; yea its mould or ground hath such a vertue, that, if it be carried to places where Mice and Rats abound, it will presently kill them; which hath often times been proved.'*[5] It is said that folk came from Dunrossness in South Mainland to fetch earth to place beneath corn stacks to ward off rats and mice.[6]

In the distant past the isolation of Havera and the fact that there is only one safe landing beach, at Nort Ham, had a possible advantage. One hundred years before Leigh's visit, in a rumbustious age, Havera was occupied by one of Shetland's more colourful characters – Ola Sinclair (about 1510) of Havera and Broo, the Great Foud (or governor). His father, Henry Sinclair, may have been born on Havera about 1488 and his is the earliest name we have that is attached to the island.

However, with its fertility, it was no doubt occupied long before that for there are traces of what might be Neolithic field boundaries and a chambered cairn, which would represent the very earliest records of habitation several thousand years ago. There is also, by the old school, the outline of what may have been a longhouse. Occupation during the Norse period is also supported by several Old Norse place names among the many derived from Scots.

Just to the north of Nort Ham is a *geo* known as Sinclair's Stove, which may be (ON) *'stofa'*, house, and may have been near the site for the Sinclair home? There are no traces of a large house now but that is the case for many houses of this period in Shetland.

Remains of chambered cairn with Foula on the horizon

"Havera wis one o da, I wid say, was as good as whit's in Shetland. You could tak a ploo an ploo da whole lot up. Der no place in dis isles [Shetland] at's laek dat: hit's jöst bits a patches here an dere, Shetland. You could tak a horse an ploo da whole lot up fae wan end tae da other. Hit wis entirely clean [not stony or weed-infested]."
Gideon Williamson (1912-1999)[4]

Around 1550, Ola left Havera and settled at Broo. Then, in 1571, the infamous Laurence Bruce of Cultmalindie became the Great Foud. Ola was no saint but he was nothing compared to Laurence Bruce. Using his new, seemingly unfettered powers, Laurence Bruce then began 'taxing' the local fishermen by demanding a fish from each boatload sold: *'… [he] took from each of certain boats from Burray, Gulberwick, Quarff and Trondra, fishing at Havera, one cod and one ling, and a further cod and ling was taken when these boats came to their merchants in Scalloway.'*[7] This does not suggest that Bruce was taking from 'Havera' boats, if there were any. The island and the Peerie Isles may not have been fishing communities at that point around 1570.

Once Ola Sinclair had departed, we do not know whether or not Havera retained some population, but Leigh observed on his visit in 1654 that Havera was *'an inhabited island'*.[8] Births were not officially recorded until a century later when an Ursula Smith was born in Havera in 1762. She may have been the last of the udal occupiers or the forerunner of what became a rapidly increasing population under the feudal laws of Scotland.

Enforced settlement

There is a traditional tale of how Havera became the property of the Bruce family of Shetland landowners and the retribution taken by the 'cheated' udal islanders. In fact, there are several versions of this tale! However, intriguing as it is, it cannot be entirely true. A wily laird is said to have literally seized Havera under feudal law by possessing its stone and earth as proof of ownership. John Williamson (1907) told a story of a Bruce arriving on the island at a time when there were udaller fisherman and families living there. On a day when the men were away fishing he was taken into a house by the senior fisherman's wife whom he requested to take a spoon into the yard and dig him up some earth and stone and give it to him. She thought it a strange request but complied and then he told her that under Scots law the island now belonged to him. The fisherman, a Smith man, returned at this point and when told what had happened said to the laird that as he was now his servant he would take him back to the mainland. The fisherman's son followed in another boat on the instructions of his father who, with the laird on board, deliberately ran his boat onto a reef at the south end of the Holm of Maywick. His son rescued him but they left the laird to drown … the reef then became known as Bruce's Baa.[9]

In a second version of the drowning, Bruce sent his son to collect the rent. When this was done the islanders took the young man back to the mainland in an old boat. Accompanying them was either another boat of theirs or, depending on the source of the story, a boat from Maywick. The old boat was then 'wrecked' on the Baa. The standby boat picked up the Havera men and they left the son of the laird to drown. There is yet a third version, which states

Old school (right) and perhaps site of Sinclair's Stove

that it was the raising of the rent by the landowner that initiated the drowning of the laird.

However, despite the stories, it seems that John Bruce of Symbister (Whalsay), legitimately took ownership of the Bigton estate that included Havera, when he married Clementina Stewart of Bigton in 1744.

Nonetheless, it is clear that something dramatic happened in the time of the Bruces to give the reef its name. But if the islanders had deliberately drowned the laird or his son there surely would have been a court case and a written record, and the men involved would have paid dearly for their actions. Perhaps there was an accidental drowning of a Bruce. There is no doubt that many Shetland

lairds were resented, if not hated at that time and putting one over on them would have been a tale to be remembered and retold many times. In the case of Havera, the resentment may have come from the action of the Bruce laird who appears to have settled the fishing families there in the late 18th century, displacing them from elsewhere; some of whom are said to have come from the Garths Banks area of Dunrossness.[10]

That several families were settled in the 18th century is supported by the fact that many of the place names of Havera have a Scottish, rather than Old Norse, origin. It is as if the old names were lost for few now knew them. Further evidence for settlement of more than one family in the 18th century is a barn of that period which was built with two entrances, two *njuggelsteyns* (on which oats were threshed) and two *gliggs* (holes in the wall through which were passed the sheaves of oats from the yard). This well−built structure was designed to be shared by more than one family. It is on Da Yard close by the site where the corn stacks were built on top of a base of large stones. It was the practice, when the sheaves were all removed for threshing, to pile the stones in the centre to prevent them becoming grown over with grass, thereby removing their effectiveness as a dry base. At Havera it seems this was done after the last harvest and there the waiting stones remain. Another unusual feature of one of the byres by the houses − an indication of the importance of sea−driven timber to such a community − is a slot, like a narrow window midway up the gable, through which timbers could be slid onto the rafters.

This was a time when many lairds insisted that fishing for the estate was part of the condition of tenancy. It was a profitable business as, generally, the catch had to be sold to them on their terms. So all over Shetland new crofts were being created to support more fishermen. The occupation of Havera at that time was all about fishing and wherever the people came from they would have had to have been fishermen.

It was at this time, it appears, that John Bruce, the laird, set up two small croft units on the nearby and much larger St Ninian's Isle and five on Havera, so forcing those 'settled' on the latter to fish for their living.[11] This could explain the simultaneous presence on Havera of four couples with young families (see family trees in Appendices), just when Parish records commenced. Of those, James Smith (1774) was the only one definitely born on the island and who may have been a relation of Ursula Smith (1762), born on the island at a similar time. James'

'Double' barn, *njugglesteyn* (white with lichen) and *gligg*

wife was Barbara Manson (1785) from Channerwick. Of the origins of the other three families – all the men with the surname Jamieson – we only know with certainty that one of the seven (there was a second marriage for one) was from Burra.

The first Jamieson couple was George Jamieson (before 1772), who married Ursula Smith (1770), but apparently not the one above from Havera. He appears to have died very shortly after the birth of their only son, Oliver Jamieson (1792). Ursula then left Havera, married and then returned by 1841 with her second husband, Walter Williamson (1765), from Dunrossness, and six or seven children. Their son, David (1800) then took up one of the five crofts and began the Williamson line on the island. The second Jamieson couple was another George Jamieson (1765) with his wife Helen (née Smith 1767) and the third couple was John Jamieson (1771) and his wife Ann (née Sinclair, about 1770). Ann died in 1819 and John married again, to Marion Jamieson (1785) from Burra. These couples made up the 'founding' families from whom the present owners and the siblings, Jessie (1903), John (1905) and Gideon (1912) Williamson – who recorded their recollections of life on the island – and May Jane Ward (1914), are descended.

There are some curious facts about these couples. Firstly, they had surnames in common, such as Smith and Jamieson, and so perhaps some were related? Secondly, their ages were very similar and the firstborn of the three Jamieson families arrived within just a few years of each other, in 1791, 1792 and 1799. Thirdly, both surnames, Sinclair and Smith, are linked with Havera. Could one, two or all three of the wives of the Jamieson men have had Havera origins or connections? Whatever their original relationships and origins, however, these families, by intermarriage through the generations, became increasingly interrelated.

Da Yard, stone base for stacks, kiln and slot in the gable

TWO

HAEM AND RIG

Haem

You could caa hit a huddle, or livin
on tap o een anidder, da wye wir hooses
wis set sae clos, een fornenst da tidder,

an aa but hingin affa da banks
wi naethin but a trenkie afore da drap,
an da dunder o da ocean anunder wis.

You could winder foo we didna faa oot,
laid heads ta traas an sidey–for–sidey.
We nivver sindered, aye baed roondaboot.

In coorse wadder, froad an brennastyooch
wheeft owre da isle; saat glansed apö
window–sheeks, waar laandit apö da röf.

Hit wis as if dey wir a caim encirclin,
begirdin wis lik kale wintered i da crub.
Maistlins da gael's splore liftit up an owre.

"We hed a dresser, a boannie dresser, an we hed a kyist o draawers … a big kyist o draawers … dan we hed a big press dat held da aetables. An dat wis really whit wis in da but end. I [in] da ben end wis dooble beds. Sae dey wir plaenty o beds. I da but bedroom dey wir twa beds, an wan een at da end…. dey wir twa o wis in a bed … some o dem hed tree but we always hed twa."
Jessie

That all four couples were settled on Havera at the same time would explain why the township on Havera appears planned and, instead of individual kilns at the end of each barn (as everywhere else in Shetland), there is a communal kiln. It also may explain why the community was so close, as Jessie said: *"Ivery hoose hed ta ken whit da nixt hoose wis döin. Hit wis laek wan hoose. Hit wisna laek iveryboady didna hae a hoose tae demsels … hit wis wan hoose."*

Those who left in 1923 spoke of their new houses on Burra as being poor compared to those they had left on Havera. However, the Havera houses had been improved in the late 1800s. Though they still basically consisted of a but, ben and closet, the walls were heightened, the roofs felted – as tar became available as a by–product of the gasworks in Lerwick – and they were possibly provided with wooden floors. Up to that point they had been thatched as everywhere else in Shetland. This may be evidence of the relative wealth of the island. They had oil–cloth on the floor of the houses when baiting haddock lines, no carpets of course and there were no dry–closets. As the houses were considered to be good it might be thought there was a fine space for everyone. However, in addition to family members there were also lodgers as servants and fishermen. For example the household of George (1820) and Mary (1822) Jamieson in 1851 included their three little boys and in addition, three adult female servants and a fisherman.

The township is at the south end of the island at the base of a narrow peninsula they called Da Yard, a short distance from the landing beach and separated from the rest of the island by a dyke. Although very close to the cliff edge the houses were surprisingly sheltered. There is a walled yard adjacent to the houses and another near the *rigs*; the latter possibly the site of a previous single large farm on the island, prior to the settlement of the families.

There was no fencing on the island but just one hill dyke that divided it in two, keeping animals out of the arable land during the growing season. That all the families were settled at the same time might also explain why the arable land was shared out so equitably and why it appears that the community was so co–operative from the beginning; though all Shetland townships had to be co–operative at that time. The division of the arable land was into three lots of 3 acres and two of 4.5 acres – which later became four crofts – though on the area that they cultivated this division is said to have been nominal. At that time the system was *runrig*: people had their acreage but it was split up taking in areas of both the best and poorest ground, while it might not be the same piece of ground from year to year. In the 19th century the landlords in Shetland rationalised the *runrig* system, giving each crofter a specific area (planking) of arable land, and at the same time often pulling down the townships and redistributing the houses to each piece of land. This never happened on Havera: the township was left and the land was never planked.

The township of Havera today with Fair Isle on the horizon and c1900

Hill dyke

Da rigs o Havera

O da boannie rigs o Havera ran
fae da Yerd tae Sinclair's Stofa.
Dey rekkit owre Da Ness an aa,
an some wis aedged wi smora.

An we muckit an we delled
An we harrowed an we singilt
An we we dippilt an we haepit
An we shaerd an we hirdit.

O we muckit an we delled
Da Big Rigs
Da Black Rigs
Da Barkiland
Da Skerpaks

An we harrowed an we singilt
Da Backlands
Da Kingmins
Da Gubb an
Da Toobies

An we we dippilt an we haepit
Da Knowe Rigs
Da Hoolaplanks
Da Smaagut rigs

An we shaerd an we hirdit
Da Lime Pows
Da Booth Rigs an aa
Da Pecrie Wirlds.

O da boannie rigs o Havera ran
fae da Yerd tae Sinclair's Stofa.
Dey rekkit owre Da Ness an aa,
an some wis aedged wi smora.

An we muckit an we delled
An we harrowed an we singilt
An we we dippilt an we haepit
An we shaerd an we hirdit.

Rig Names:

Da Cutts (Nort, Mid and Hame)
Da Barkiland (Nort, Mid and Hame)
Da Lime Pows (Three)
Da Booth Lands
Da Peerie Wirlds
Da Red Knowe
Da Yeoolaplank
Da Skerpaks
Da Backlands
Sklate Roof
Da Kingmins
Da Gubb
Da Toobies
Da Shade
Da Baltastoor
Da Hoolaplanks
Da Knowie Rigs
Da Steep Rig
Da Kokkiloori
Da Ooter Delling
Da Big Rigs
Da Black Rigs
Da Smaagut Rigs
Da Hankys (Peerie, Mid and Muckle)

"Weel, see, [they] … hed whit dey caa'd 'rigs': bits o strips here an strips dere. Wan, two, tree, fowr – dey wir fowr crofts … dan dey jöst pairtit oot: du hed a bit here, an dan hit wis aa spread oot, du sees. Hit wisna, du kens, sam as wan croft – dey didna wirk hit dat wye: hit wisna whit you caa'd 'plankit' – he wisna plankit …I tink da idee wis, see, dey wid divide hit oot evenly. Der wir better laand some places as others, du sees."
Gideon

The soil of Havera produced good harvests of potatoes, bere and oats, with each strip – a reflection of their importance to the families – having a name. The *rigs* themselves may have faded from the landscape but the names remain.

Da Waster Isle

We ösed ta sweem da kye dere ivery simmer:
fat quaigs, faert an filskit fae da dookin.
Dey buldered up da banks niffin da sweet girse.

Bi winter dey wir ready for da byre's saaft poans;
bairns wi watter, shappit neeps an hay. Neist voar
dey wir apö da hill, lowsed fae veggel–baands.

But whitna onkerry wi wir yowes. Slippin rams
in winter apö da Waster Isle wis sic a bassel.
If da sea wis barmin we took wir chance; waited till

Taing Skerry drappt her gaerd, dan nippit trowe,
höved a ram ashore, een ivery time, watcht dem
scale da banks, der cöts aa but mirackled.

Sometimes we nivver got dem haem till May.
Da lichtsome time wis whin a dose o fock wid laand
ta lib da lambs or caa an roo. Someen wid bring

a bottle, someen bannocks. But whit we bafft
ta gyet sheep aff da isle: men shivvin, passin dem
doon owre rocks, men haddin da boat steady, men

heistin dem in owre, men yokkin a hadd o dem.
But Da Waster Isle wis speeshil i da simmer dim:
time stöd still. We laached an yarned an wrocht.

> *"And dan dey wir anidder smaa isle we caa'd Da Waster Isle an dat wis a fine island for da sheep. We pat da sheep in ivery simmer …. in da mont o May … an dan we took dem oot again ivery November when we wir delled up da tatties."*
> **Jessie**

The people were fairly self–sufficient in the basics. There were hens and each family had at least one milking cow and maybe a heifer and calf. In the summer, the sheep and most of the cattle were kept on the adjacent and much smaller Waster Isle, the latter being swum the quarter mile (1/2 km) or so across the sea. Waster Isle, no bigger than a large holm, was also the source of gulls' eggs; a generous bounty in the spring.

They worked the land together, digging, sowing and harvesting. No one fell behind in the cycle of the season. Bere was the first to be harvested and they cut everyone's patch together before moving on to the next task.

Fishing all year round was the main source of income, so it was the women who managed the land as well as the domestic scene, along with hired servants who were often single adult relatives or young nieces or nephews. The children too had to play their part and had regular daily tasks. Everything was carried in *kishies* for, apart from wheelbarrows, there were no wheeled vehicles or horses. So, fish from the boats, seaweed from the shore, peats from the beach to the houses, all had to be carried on their backs. Annie Deyell, a pupil–teacher on Havera around 1916, remembers that, at low tide, islanders waded out into the sea to cut the seaweed, which was later carried up the cliff path to be spread on the *rigs*.[12]

The families had peats across at Deepdale on the mainland as there was no peat on Havera. As peat–cutting coincided with busy times in the crofting and fishing cycle, they usually paid for the peats to be cut for them. However, they sailed or rowed back and fore to work the peats, raising and turning them as the summer passed. Sometimes family members who had gone to the herring stations at Sandwick would walk the hills to Deepdale to do a day's work when they had time off. The transporting of the peats off the hill was difficult and required sledges and hired ponies. They waited until after sunset to sledge the peats down the slopes as it was easier when the dew was on the ground. Annie Deyell remembers how they had to hang on to the heavy sledge full of peats to prevent it taking off down the steep slope. Then the peats had to be loaded on the boats, lying off the rocks, taken across to Havera and unloaded at Nort Ham where stacks were built above the beach. This was just one of the many tasks that had to be carried out by all available hands, merely to survive.

> *"We hed bere, dat wis for beremael; ots, for otmael, an dan dey wir taaties an neeps an kale an aa dat things. Oh, hit fairly grew. You ken, hit wis aafil göd laand, splaendit laand."*
> **Jessie**

> *"Hit was a big croft, a heavy wirkin croft. Aafil göd land, splaendit land. Ivery bit was delled oot; was aa med in rigs. Everything was delled wi a spade; an muck was kyerried on an borrowed on, an dan we hed whit we caa'd waar – seaweed – an dat wis aa kyerried fae da banks; maybe twa hunder kishies. An wan [hundred] wis kyerried up a banks at da nort side o da isle, an wan wis affa da ayre below da hooses. Sae dat was tree week's wark afore you stertit ta dell, an dat wis nearly anidder twa weeks … sae hit's haevy wark.*
>
> *We med middeens, sware middeens – man, dey wir beautiful … hed dem pattit – loavely … We [harrowed] did dat at nichts whin hit wis dark, i da darkenin. We left da harrowin for nicht … at nine o'clock hit wis he wis comin kinda dark an du could hardly see."*
> **Jessie**

Paets

Da aert wis datn göd on Havera – wi fine baess,
fat lambs – we nivver mindit dat wir paets wis awa
bi Boadi Gyo; wir hömins i da heichts o Deebdaal.

We'd cut banks ta raise an turn da simmer lang.
An whan hit cam ta tak paets haem, we browt
wir sledge an gud at nicht, for dew apö da grund

med licht o strug. Bairns i da mirknin fyaarmed
ta clim on tap. Hit took aa haands ta hadd back
a sledge apö da broo, fae tummelin owre da banks.

His wis a job loddin bags o paets inta da boat
affa da rocks, rowin or sailin haem, at times
a sunset tae da wastird dat could brack a haert.

We'd bring back firkins o caald waal watter:
you nivver missed a chance ithin da simmer.
Eence, in Clift Soond, da tail fluke o a brigdi

glufft da bairns. Dug–tired, we'd aese da oars
at Nort Ham, chain–gang wir paets up owre
da ebb. Stacks shön tooered abön da noosts.

Old School, Holm of Maywick and Deepdale

THREE

NIVVER HAANDLESS AN BAANDLESS

While the men had to be carpenters as well as fishermen, able to make a *restin-shair* or a kist, a barrow or spade handle out of sea–driven timber, or repair wear and tear to their boats, the women had to be able to bake, spin, card and knit, make clothes and *taatit-rugs* out of scraps. And when the men were no longer physically able to go offshore to the cod and ling fishing they fished inshore.

The old men also took on lighter work such as making *kishies* or accompanying the women on trips to Scalloway or Maywick for stores: no one could afford to be idle. Cash income came almost entirely from the fishing and the annual sale of wool, sheep and cattle or the occasional otterskin, but it was supplemented by the sale of knitwear, a very important activity carried out in spare moments in the summer season and particularly in the winter. Girls were taught from a very early age: Jessie recalled making a small spenser (under–garment), with the help of her grandmother, for the Papil Kirk sale when she was six. It raised 1s 6d, of which she was very proud. The women and girls used to do fancy lace–knitting, but when Fair Isle knitting became popular they concentrated on that.

Finished garments were taken to the shops at Scalloway where some would only give them goods in exchange and not cash. This system of 'truck' lasted into the early 20th century. If it was a day of weather suitable for a trip to Scalloway, all of eight miles (13 km) or so, then it was a day suitable for fishing too, so all the able–bodied men would be at sea. The women, however, were quite capable of travelling there themselves, by sail or rowing up Clift Sound, and were also well used to making the trip to Maywick, perhaps to the shop van, perhaps with a cow to the roup or to the bull. The open wooden boat would have two pairs of oars and a lug–sail and the women's hands, already toughened by croft work, would have been hardened to hours of rowing.

Leaving Nort Ham after *rooin* and shearing

"*Dey didna geeng ta nae lines, less jöst a bit o a line … for da saat fysh or onythin tae demsels. An da boys an da owld men gied ta whit we caa 'da shuttin' … dat wis da handlin … an dey got haddocks, splendeed haddocks … for da saatin; an piltocks.*"
Jessie.

"*We med aa dis fancy stoles –'cloods' we caa'd dem – an scarfs an fancy haps wi fancy boarders an fancy middles. We med aa dat, an da onythin A'm vexed aboot- dat I didna keep aa dat owld patterns … I hae a few o dem … dan dat stoppit. Den we gud on tae da hosiery … dis Fair Isles. Dat pat a stop tae da fancy eens for dey [shops] widna buy dem. Dat gud on da whole winter. But in simmer dey wirna much time ta mak. Wance you stertit da Voar wark dey wir aafil little time ta mak. … We cairdit an span too. But hit wis mainly for socks an boys' jimpirs … maybe twartree jimpirs ida year … hit wis aa natural … we nivver dyed none. We mixed da white wi da black an med grey.*"
Jessie

"We took da goods [knitted garments] ta Scallowa. We aalways gud to Scallowa ... a boat lodd o hit. But we gied owre tae da mainland tae Maywick, an da [shop] vans came dere ... in simmer but no in winter ... couldna land in winter. An when we wrowt in da paets we gud owre da hill for da [Sandwick] vans."
Jessie

Everything and everybody leaving the island and everything and everybody arriving had to come across the Nort Ham shore: from the export of fish to the import of peats; from the post, to the teacher or the occasional minister, nurse but rarely doctor; to the carriage of knitwear to the shops and the return with tea or sugar from their shelves. Luckily the narrow entrance to Nort Ham has a southeast aspect, somewhat sheltered by the mainland. Without this relatively rock−free *geo* and beach Havera could never have been inhabited. Notwithstanding reasonable access and shelter, there were many times when weather and sea were such that they could not

"But da wye dey did on da Isle, if I was short o sugar ... dis hoose ... an da next hoose was short o somethin idder ... you nivver keepit hit tae yourself, you pairtit hit even among you, afore dey wir naethin left."
Jessie

Nort Ham

Sailin for da airrands

Da shop van cam ta Maywick but, if hit luikit
lik we could mak Scallawa, wis weemen fock
wid rise aerly an set aff. A aald man wid tag

alang as skipper or, mair lik, draemin o a dram.
We'd rig wis head ta fit in oilskins. Ta starboard
da Clift Hills paced wis, lowerin. We skiled

for flans at wheeft black fantin oot o naewye.
Hit wis a race ta gyet da lugsail doon afore
dey strack, dan heist him up again an on wir wye.

Ivery een o wis hed a pack o makkin: spencers,
glivs, ganseys, haps. An whit a argie−bargie ta fin
whit dey'd fetch ta set fornenst a aer o shuggar,

saat, tae, paraffin, matches, sopp. Dan, if dey wir
ony penga, someen micht buy bain for mendin
böts, or maybe flannel an a ribbeen for da bairns;

some clowes, black plug. In simmer, we'd lay in
aetmeal an flooer ta fill da girnal till da hairst.
Apö da wye back, mair as lik da man wid be

da waar o drink, swinklan i da tilfers, an we'd tak
da helm nae budder. Clift Soond wis a lang row
if da wind dilled. On Havera, wir fock wid keep

a wadder eye, meet wis at Nort Ham, kerry
wir kishies for wis. Da bairns luikit for sweeties,
da aald men wid settle wi da paeper an a pipe.

Robert Jamieson (1875) sailing to Scalloway, with the lug sail; decked fishing boats moored ahead

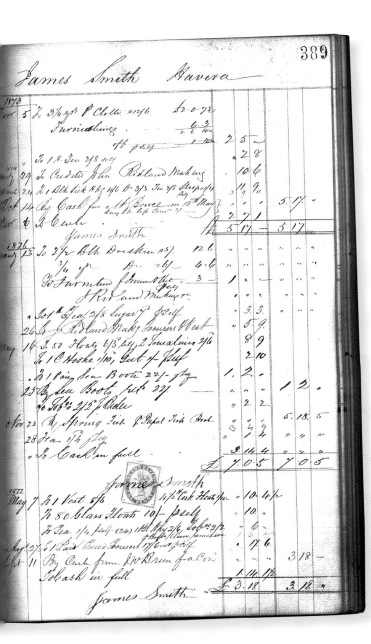

1873-1877 Hay & Co Scalloway shop book for James Smith (1824)[13] courtesy of Shetland Museum and Archives

Hame Ham

get out for supplies for days, and when the time came towards the end when there were few able-bodied men on the island, isolation could last for weeks. When this happened they shared the supplies they had.

The main food commodities they bought were sugar and tea and sometimes loaves of bread. In the summer they could get to Maywick too but in the winter because of the swell it was usually impossible to land on the beach there. Their winter diet was not so varied as summer, but they had their dried fish and usually *reestit* mutton, salt beef and pork from killing a cow or pig. Sailing up Clift Sound can be a dangerous activity and the woman skipper had to keep a weather eye and have the sail down sharply if need be if the boat was not to be overturned. Sometimes, older men no longer hale enough for the fishing would accompany the women to Scalloway, perhaps insisting that their experience was needed. But the chances were, after a few hours in Scalloway, that they would be incapable of a sober opinion on the way home!

"All our shopping was done in Scalloway, eight miles away. We had a small boat with a dipping lug sail, but if the wind was contrary we had to row. At first I held the oars too tightly and my palms were continually blistered, but as time went on I learned to row and steer like a native, and, if we were sailing, to watch for the black flan crossing the water from the Clift Hills, and help to get the sail down without it touching the sea before the flan hit us. The old lady [Barbara Jamieson 1849] who lived in the house over the cave was usually the skipper. We had some perilous voyages, and would become soaked in spite of oilskins. Once or twice we had difficulty making the little landing place."
Annie Deyell[14]

FOUR

WIND AND WATTER

Watter

Watter: nane can live ithoot hit. On Havera
dey wir mony a dry simmer, a weet winter.
Faests an fantins: we hed ta hain apön hit.

Nae richt burns, nae peerie lochs, nae shuns,
nae watery höls. Da isle wis limey an dry,
but green as green. Ivery drap o watter wis

a prisoner. You wasted nane: you wöshed
da laem dan mopped da oilcloth, slooshed
da briggisteyns. We filt a barrel fae da rain

at fell apö da röf, mony a kyettle fae da rones.
We fetched watter wi kegs apö wir backs:
dat wye we didna spill a drap. Da waal wis

up da broo, aside da mill. Hit wis lichtsome
wark in simmer, a scunner i da winter.
We nivver gud aff da isle ithoot a firkin ta fill:

ta quilk an quilk dat clean, caald draucht
wis bliss in simmer; nae haddin back.
Wir kye tör dewy girss but, eence i da byre,

we hed ta watter dem. Dey wir anidder waal
at Haem Ham but only for da baess. Hit wis
owre near da runniks ta be kirsen. At ebbin tide

bairns wid rin ta catch da spring at Gatni Gyos;
tak a yoag shall ta fill a daffik, peerie little
bi peerie little: dey wir somethin magic

aboot fresh watter owsin i da ocean's face.
Hit wis a fine neebrid for wir planti—crubs.
Havera wis limey an dry, but green as green.

Havera is so small that there are no burns. Its highest point is in the centre of the island and, curiously, that is where the well is located and from where the islanders carried water in kegs on their backs to their homes. There are one or two springs on the coast. One lies on the path down to Hame Ham; however, as the water might be contaminated by run−off from the byres, it was not used for human consumption. Another is on the north side of the island, down a *geo*. In times of drought, children were sometimes sent to collect fresh water from a rocky shore − using a scallop shell to scoop it up from a pool − or fresh water was brought back from Burra or the mainland; a time−consuming exercise. Annie Deyell said that she used rainwater off the roof.

With no running water there could be no water mill, so the grain was ground on a quern, often a child's daily chore. Sometimes it was taken to Longhill at Maywick and ground in the water mill there.[15] Grain was a staple of their diet. Jessie said: *"We hed a whern at da end o a shed …an dan whan da mael cam short* [ran out] *we hed ta grind on da whern … hit wis heavy goin!"* The women were constantly baking for they ate oatmeal and beremeal in one form or another daily.

When the big water mill was built in Central Mainland at Weisdale in 1855, the Havera folk took their grain in sacks to Scalloway where it was taken on by horse and cart. This was not only time−consuming but cost money. Shetland people, however, are inveterate problem solvers and an answer was found that it was hoped would save them time, effort and expense. And it probably came about through happenstance.

In 1848 Jane Laurenson (1821) of Bressay married Oliver Smith (1811) of Havera. There must have been a close connection between the Laurensons and the island as Jane's step−sister was recorded as a

> *"[We baked] ivery blissit day, an some days twice. … We bakit on a iron, wi 'taes', fowr taes, an da colls wis pitten underneath dere … Aafil göd bannocks … fine smell wi hit … an dan we hed pans dat we bakit in … whit we caa'd pan brönnies … jöst oardinary pans you fried in. We hed a Dutch oaven tö. We bakit i da big oaven tö … aa on da oppen fire."*
> **Jessie**

house servant in the Smith family in the 1851 census. Then, in 1852, another sister, Catherine (1830) married Thomas Williamson (1829), also of Havera. Although the latter couple did not live on the island, the former did. Possibly not long after, perhaps in 1866 when his wife died – the year the wind mill was built – the girls' father, James Laurenson (1797), a stonemason, moved from Bressay to live with Jane and family on Havera (where he died in 1871). A few years earlier in 1859, a brother of the girls, Gifford Laurenson (1828), a mason like his father, was employed by the Society of Antiquaries in Edinburgh to repair the broch of Mousa, described at the time as *'mouldering into dust'*[16]. Gifford built a miniature of the broch for the Society, which is still in the National Museum of Scotland in Edinburgh today.

It is entirely plausible that it was Gifford or his father James who came up with the idea of how to solve the problem of milling grain on Havera. Perhaps Gifford was on Havera visiting his sister Jane and his father when the discussion turned to the lack of a water mill and Gifford suggested a wind mill! There were no wind mills on Shetland, for there had always been an ample supply of water to provide the power for the single axle click−mill that provided the simple, elegant and durable solution for turning the small mill stone.

Island tradition has it[17] that a Fleming Laurenson and a man from Dunrossness built the wind mill. In fact, James Laurenson had a brother and another son both named Fleming, one of whom must have been present on Havera at the time for his unusual name to be remembered. As James would have been 69 at this time he would have been able to give advice but little more. The mill is a circular building, unusual for Shetland, and very broch–like, even to the regularly spaced openings for a boom–cum–axle high up in its wall (reminiscent of the internal openings of a broch): a shape with which Gifford had recently become very familiar. So it is entirely plausible that Gifford influenced the design. However, the workmanship is not up to the standard of a stonemason, which supports the story that it was built by his brother Fleming and a Dunrossness man.

The exact mechanism of the mill, sadly long gone, is not known but the boom, which projected horizontally through one of the holes – depending on wind direction – supported a wind vane. This consisted of slatted wood from which individual slats could be removed if the wind was too strong. The boom projected below the height of the milling apparatus, which was supported by a stout floor more than halfway up the tower. There was no gearing[18] so presumably power was transferred to the grinding stone by means of a rope or belt. Unfortunately, the system did not work very well and the wind mill was not used for very long. After that, grain was once again taken to Weisdale and then also to the more accessible Quendale Mill in South Mainland when it was built in 1867. However, the Havera mill went on to serve another convenient purpose. It became a very visible point on which to drape a white sheet to attract attention when needed. Today, the wind mill tower on Havera is a fine landmark, perched on the top of the island, just like a miniature broch.

Interior of windmill

Plan of the windmill

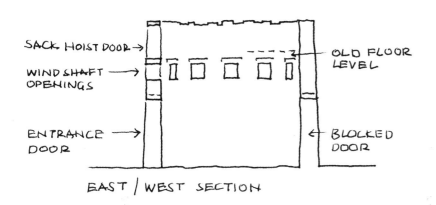

SACK HOIST DOOR →

WINDSHAFT OPENINGS →

ENTRANCE DOOR →

OLD FLOOR LEVEL

← BLOCKED DOOR

EAST / WEST SECTION

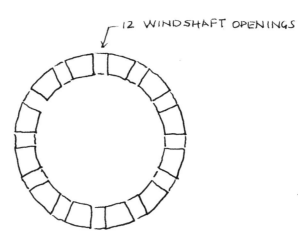

12 WINDSHAFT OPENINGS

WINDSHAFT LEVEL PLAN

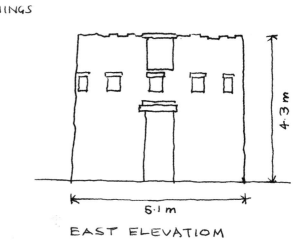

4·3 m

5·1 m

EAST ELEVATIOM

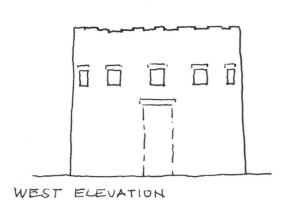

WEST ELEVATION

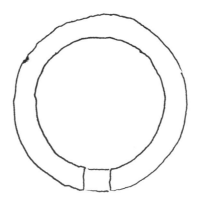

SACK HOIST DOOR PLAN

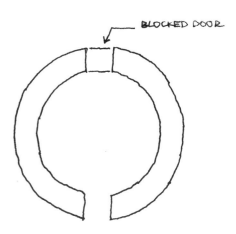

BLOCKED DOOR

GROUND FLOOR PLAN

Da windmill

Da only windmill ithin da hael o Shetland
an Havera hed hit. Weel, dey wir nae burns,
but a stoor o wind. Hit seemed a göd idee.

Fae a distance hit could be a Martello Too'er,
a peerie broch, or doocot; a kinda loadstar
for whaar you wir; an maybe whaa you wir.

Da sails wis only ösed whin grindin coarn;
we could möv dem richt aroond da too'er,
dependin on da ert. But, dey wir wint ta say

hit wis mair ös as meid dan mill. An feth,
we needed meids. Ithin ill wadder hit wis
a gödless sklent o watter: teckin bi Crö Taing,

Rivek's Baa, Taing Skerry an aa da deevilry
an danger aroond da Waster Isle. Or rowin
haem ithin da mirknin fae Burra, Quarff.

Hit's still a place wirt seekin, a laandmark
i da haert o Havera; fin your bearins dere,
link tae a uncan wirld, a waavelin horizon.

Da Windmill

Pauleen Wiseman

FIVE

A SEA HAIRST

The *Ann,* courtesy of Shetland Museum and Archives

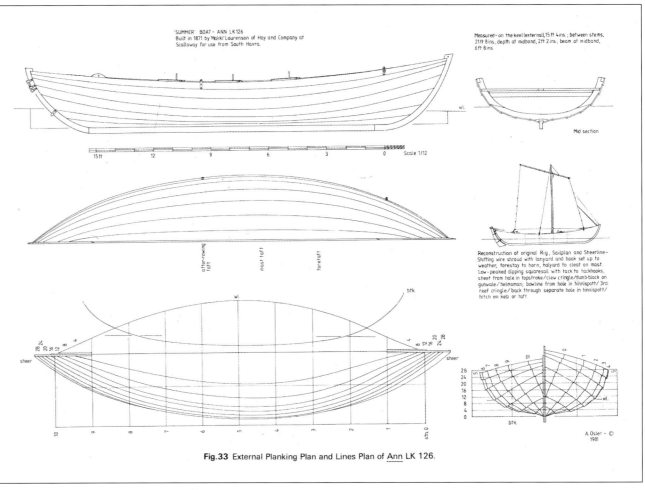

'SUMMER' BOAT - ANN LK 126
Built in 1871 by 'Makki' Laurenson of Hay and Company at
Scalloway for use from South Havra.

Measured - on the keel (external), 15 ft 4 ins.; between stems,
21 ft 8 ins, depth at midband, 2 ft 2 ins.; beam at midband,
6 ft 8 ins.

Mid section

Reconstruction of original Rig, Sailplan and Sheerline -
Shifting wire shroud with lanyard and hook set up to
weather, forestay to horn, halyard to cleat on mast.
Low-peaked dipping squaresail with tack to tackhooks,
sheet from hole in topstroke / clew cringle / dumb-block on
gunwale / helmsman; bowline from hole in hinnispott / 3rd.
reef cringle / back through separate hole in hinnispott /
hitch on keb or taft.

A. Osler - ©
1981

Fig.33 External Planking Plan and Lines Plan of Ann LK 126.

Plan of the *Ann*, Osler (1983)[19]

> *"Dey used yon beach* [Hame Ham] *a lot when dey wir goin tae da fishin becaas hit wis haandy wi da hooses. … Dey said dey hed, dey wir laekly used wi hit, dey said even wi da sea* [a stormy sea], *a fellow said dey jöst surfed in sometimes. Nearly impossible."*
> **Gideon**

Mindin on gyaain
tae da haaf

I mind da first time da men took me tae da haaf.
Hit wis fine gyaain, for dey wir a stoor o wind.
I da mid–room I shurley baitit miles o towes.

Da best time wis whan aa wir lines wis shut.
I was sent forrard for da fire kyettle an da maet.
I boiled a dose o fysh; we hed brönnies wi

fresh butter an a keg o blaand. Dan da hailin:
I kavveled on till no fit ta pyaa; fingers numb
an stivvened. Fat tusk bummeled i da shott.

We nivver med for haem till da darknin an
dey wir nae let up, less a peerie neeb fae time
ta time. Guttin, owsin, an dan da wind dilled

an we hed ta row. I shurley rockit meesel
ta sleep, matchin da stroke. Dey said I tippit aff
da taft, lay wavvelin ithin da cradle o da cod.

I kent naethin o hit till someen set me doon apö
da beach. Da haaf men, dey wir göd–haertit
an kindly, an nivver cöst hit up ta me again.

Havera wis lichtsome wi extry fock at lodged
here for da simmer: ivery hoose prammed tae da
gunwales; lodges at da gyos. Six men tae a boat

an a dose ta varg apö da beach. At nicht dey'd be
music an maybe coortin: a simmer blink, a reesel
o cotts, a hinny–spot, a antrin mirry–begyit.

49

Fishing by line for cod and ling was an important pursuit near–shore off the Scalloway islands in the 16th century – easy pickings for the Great Foud Laurence Bruce. In the 1790s it was recorded that there were about 200 fishing boats in Dunrossness, mainly large six–oared *sixerns*, six–oared yoals and smaller four–oared *fourerns*, and that *'Burra, Havera and Papa* [had] *28 smaller boats'*.[20] As the Burra *haaf* (fishing grounds) off the Scalloway islands is much closer to the shore than elsewhere in Shetland, there was no need for the large *sixerns*. Such boats, at about 25–27 feet (8–9 m) overall, were used for fishing when the distances were up to 40 miles (64 km) offshore. In the early 18th century there are records of fishing stations for drying cod (usually stony beaches) on the Peerie Isles – Oxna, Papa, Linga, Langa and Hildasay – but not for Havera.[21] The apparent lack of a fishing station at that time on Havera fits with the suggestion that it was not until after the mid–18th century that families were settled there by the laird. It is the case also that the Peerie Isles are relatively flat with suitable landing and drying beaches, whereas Havera is almost entirely cliff–bound.

By the 1851 census of the Peerie Isles there were three families on Oxna, one on Linga, two on Papa and three on Hildasay. This gave a total of around 60 permanent residents and 24 servants and seasonal fishermen on the four islands, while on Havera alone that year there were five families made up of 35 residents plus 8 servants and seasonal fishermen.

On either side of the township on Havera, within just a few metres, are cliffs. To the immediate southeast is The Harbour, but it was no safe haven for boats; besides, it has no easy access to its shore. Immediately to the west is Hame Ham, which has a steep path to the beach. But neither is Hame Ham a very safe place for boats, being filled with rocks and shoals while the sea can run right up to the

Summer boats drawn up on the Nort Ham beach

base of the cliff. Nevertheless, it was closer to the houses than the only safe landing (at Nort Ham) and apparently was used by the men when fishing. If they ran in there in poor weather they must have been as familiar with its safe passages as the deeply–ingrained lines on the palms of their hands.

The boats, which were their lifeline, were kept at Nort Ham, which lay a short distance to the northeast of the township. This was the only place in the island where they could be pulled well above the worst of the winter weather. The only other regular 'landing' on the isle was adjacent to the fish–drying beach on the west side at Skeo Geos where fresh caught fish were offloaded onto the rocks.

It was reckoned that there were at least two boats to each of the five households on Havera, one for the summer cod and the second for haddock. Then, in addition, there were two relatively large boats, around 24 feet (8 m) overall and these were used for jobs such as transporting peats. The boats used for cod and ling at the summer *haaf* were nearer 21 feet (7 m) overall, and as Gideon Williamson said: *"dey used ta caa dem 'simmer boats' at wis gyaain tae da fishin. Dey gud a lang distance i da simmer time."* The even smaller *fourerns* were used for inshore haddock fishing right through the year.

"From around 1850 the haddock fishery had been firmly established at a few places in Shetland notably around

Scalloway and Burra. A special type of boat suitable for this fishery had evolved known simply as a haddock boat … an open boat 13 feet long in keel – a smaller version of the sixern – and propelled by a square sail and two pairs of oars.[22]

Incredibly, one of Havera's summer cod boats, the *Ann*, survives. She has been extensively rebuilt and repainted in her original colours in the Shetland Museum boatshed. She was built by Malcolm Laurenson in Scalloway in 1871 for David and Robert Williamson and named after the latter's daughter, Ann Jane Williamson (1858). The boat reputedly cost £6.10s, is 21 foot 8 inches (7 m) overall and was crewed by three men. She is Shetland's second oldest extant boat and the only surviving example of this type used from Bigton to Burra in those days. After her fishing days she was used from East Burra where the family had settled after leaving the island and was last used around 1960. Sadly, her final employment ashore was for tarring the bottom rope of herring drift–nets. Tar was poured into her and the long rope passed through from end to end but as it happened, this helped preserve her timbers. Providentially, in 1981, a plan of her was drawn up and so her restoration has been entirely accurate.[23]

The cod and ling fishing ground was not far offshore and they did not have to stay out overnight, so if bad weather sprang up, the lines – which were around 300 feet (100 m) long with baited hooks every 30 feet (10 m) – could be left and retrieved later. Havera has very limited areas of stony beach on which the catch was dried after gutting and splitting, so an artificial 'beach' of stone was created above Skeo Geos. Nearby are stone ruins, most likely a chambered cairn, but which were thought to be the remains of the salt store. When fish were brought ashore it was usually the old men and the boys who salted them and spread them on the stones and the

The *Ann* restored

latter would often also have the task of watching over them to keep off the gulls. When dried, the fish would be taken to Burra or Scalloway to be sold for cash. It was said that the *Ann*, under sail, once travelled the eight miles (13 km) to Scalloway in an hour.

Another, much lesser, harvest from the sea, were otters. In the area of Skeo Geos there are the remains of at least one and perhaps two or three stone otter traps. The animals were killed and skinned and their pelts sold, particularly around 1900, when a good price could be got for them south where they were used in the ladies' fashion industry.

"From the west side we came home nearly every day to have one meal and then go back. This is what made it such slavery. More than half our time was taken up in coming and going."
Andrew Jamieson.[24]

Da Ann

LK126

Skilled haands beelt me as a simmer boat; lean,
sea—faerdy. I med da winter boats luik smaa,
da sixerns bördly, wir flit boats bulderin.

Noostit tagidder, navy abön an maroon below,
we wir a sicht wirt seein. Whin dey took me ta
da isle, dat first time, fock left der rigs ta luik.

I cut bi Kettlaness lik a neesik, mi new sails foo,
mi iron rövs glinkin lik scores o diamonds.
Wir Ann Jean ran ta Nort Ham ta hansel me.

Foo mony score o olicks im I kyerried?
Foo mony pair o böts is climmed in owre me?
Foo mony brides skurtit, foo mony kirknin couples?

Mony's da time A'm felt da linns anunder me,
mi sclates poo'in fornenst da kabe, da rooth.
A'm kyerried dem aa: a janderin coo, a halliget ram.

Da hidmost time dey noostit me, up high for winter,
dat micht a bön da end. But, na, mi boo wis tippit up;
wir men filt mi starn foo o tar – twa hale barrels o hit –

dan hauled der bush ropes trowe da claggy pöl.
Dey fekkit oot da lines apö da beach, tar skeetchin
aawye till dey wir klined. Fock cut dem fae der oilskins,

brunt der terry claes. Da peerie boys widna tak paes:
dey watcht da men, windered if dey tö micht
be herrin men; sail da drifters fae Papil, Scallowa.

A'm ootlestit nearly aa da widden boats; but noo
anidder kindly haand is mizzered me, browt me back
ta life; felt ivery lith o mi riggy. A'm göd as new.

Da Ann

Pauleen Wiseman

Mindin on da beach–boys

I sit noo, neebin owre wir fire an mind apön
da life A'm hed. At twal year aald, six boys
we wir, wirkin wi da men. A sixern wid come

an we'd help unlodd her. Shoremen wid takk
a tully tae tusk apö da spleetin–boards an swing
da bismar. Wir fingers sweed ithin da vats o saat,

layerin da fysh. Five days afore we swilled dem,
dan laid dem oot apö da Skyuggies beach ta drain
or up owre da banks whaar we wir roogit stanes.

Afore nicht, we hed ta gadder dem tagidder,
cover dem. I da moarnin, barefit, we'd spang
fae ee steepel tae da neist, spreadin an turnin cod,

aye watchin for rain.   Dey wir weel–shrucken
bi da end o hit: a bloom, a crump o saat. We likkit
kyempin, wis beach–boys. Minds–du, dat wis da days!

Skeo Geos

53

That time was taken to build these traps suggests that otters were regular visitors to Havera: they do have a taste for fish!

Virtually all the Havera men and their grown boys were fishermen. In 1851, ten men of the five families were recorded as fishermen, also three lodgers and a fourteen−year old boy servant, Thomas Ewenson (1836) from Burra. His father, George Ewenson (1802), was a boat builder and had been on Havera in 1827 (when his first son was born there), presumably mending a boat. Nort Ham is a relatively narrow *geo* and it must have been a very crowded and busy place when the boats were coming and going, with long lines, oars and sails.

Fishing from Havera seems to have been very successful. *"In the Spring of 1844 Hay & Company ... arranged with the two lairds in Dunrossness, John Bruce of Sumburgh and William Bruce of Bigton - they having given up all interest in the fishing business - to handle most of the fish cured on the beaches of the South Mainland."*[25] If Bruce of Bigton had originally insisted that the Havera men fish for him this had come to an end and from 1844 they were free to sell their fish to Hay & Co. *"The catches [of cod mainly] for the early part of 1849 show the relative importance of the various westside stations. Papil came first with 797 cwts of winter fish followed by Scalloway with 684 and Hamnavoe with 597, while Nesbister produced 64 cwt and Hagrister a mere 30 cwts."*[26] Since landings from the Peerie Isles and the north end of Burra would have been at Hamnavoe or Scalloway, most of the catch landed at Papil probably came from just the south end of East and West Burra and Havera, indicating just how important the Havera fishing must have been.

Andrew Jamieson (1855), from Channerwick, spent almost three years at the fishing on Havera as a youth, around the years 1869−1871. He is recorded there as a 'general servant' on the 1871 census residing with James Smith (1824) and his sister

Otter Trap

Martha Smith (1817). In 1874 he emigrated to New Zealand on the emigrant ship *Howrah*. Luckily, late in life, he gave an account of the tough time he spent at the fishing.

That Andrew recalls mending nets suggests that the Havera men were now also fishing for herring. Andrew went on to say that he and the other boy *'returned to our homes at Channerwick.'* It may be sheer

coincidence that a Shetland companion of Andrew's on the *Howrah* in 1874 was Stewart Jamieson (1855), no relation but also from Channerwick. Stewart was the brother of James (Dey) Jamieson (1847) who married Barbara Ann (1849) of Havera and settled there. Perhaps it was Stewart who was Andrew's companion on Havera, brought there by his brother James along with Andrew?

A Hazardous Pursuit

Men were regularly lost at the fishing for storms could whip up quickly at any time of year. There were no forecasts and the fishermen were the only judges of the coming weather. The case of Walter Williamson (1811), a son of the earliest couple to be settled, was not untypical. He was Havera−born but, being a younger son had to settle his family in his wife's community on Burra. They had six children, the youngest less than a year old when the Maywick boat on which he worked was lost at the ling fishing in a winter gale of 1857. Walter drowned along with two Dunrossness men, Laurence Smith (1812) and George Leask (1811).

The body of one of the drowned fisherman was not found on the shore until July when his brother was called on to identify him. The trauma in recognising him caused the brother a mental breakdown and it took him some months to recover before he could go back in a boat and face the sea again.

Just as Walter was probably staying in Maywick with the family who owned the boat, rather than with his own family, the Havera families normally had single men and boys – like Andrew Jamieson – staying with them whom they employed for the summer *haaf* fishing. In the census of 1851 there were two Goudie men, William (1823) and Laurence (1828) from Dunrossness staying with two Jamieson families, as fishermen along with their sister Janet (1820) who was a domestic servant. As happens, four years later, one of the daughters of the Williamson household, Ann Williamson (1831) married the elder Goudie brother on Havera and left the island. She made a good choice, for he went on to become skipper of the schooner *Agatha*. In 1871 there was an American boy aged 12 recorded on the census whose origins are a mystery.

More than one man of Havera descent 'returned' to the island. By the mid 1870s James Jamieson (1841), born in Maywick but whose father was born on Havera, returned with his family to be a fisherman and boatbuilder; the latter an almost essential skill for the island. His brother, Walter Jamieson (1835),

Wife in Ston

...
Dat day
ten boats gud doon:
six fae Gloup
an een fae Fedaland
fae Haraldswick
fae Rönas Voe
an Havera.

On ivery broo
lippenen een skiled seawirds
wadder empty.

On a knowe at Gloup
der a wife in ston
glinderin

(extract of original poem)

who was born in Channerwick, also 'returned' with his family at that time. Tragically, Walter and his son, also Walter (1863), were lost off Burra with their brand new boat in the 1881 *haaf* disaster. Ten Shetland boats, comprising 58 fishermen, were lost that day. The names of both men are inscribed on the monument at Gloup, on the island of Yell, along with all the others. They were the only fishermen lost from this part of Shetland during that terrible summer gale of the 20th July, which caught so many boats at the *haaf*. When Walter got into difficulties that day, a boat, possibly the west–side Steamer, offered to take them aboard; but how could old Walter leave his new boat? He turned down the offer and he, his son and James Smith (1859) from Sandwick, the third member of the crew, paid the price. Nothing was ever seen of Walter again, but his son's body, tied to two buoys, came ashore at Banna Minn on Burra.

While Havera still had a viable community at the close of the 19th century – no doubt due to their success as fishermen and the fact that the island was endowed with a fertile soil that provided the staples of their diet, and perhaps also because it was closer to the market than some – many other islands, including the Peerie Isles, were gradually being abandoned one by one. First to be abandoned, by 1871, was Papa then Langa by 1881, Hildasay by 1891, with Linga and Oxna to follow. However, the writing was on the wall for Havera too. Success at the fishing brought the capital to invest in decked vessels just before the turn of the century. These larger fishing boats, however, could not be moored at Havera and this meant the able–bodied men were away from home during the week, leaving fewer – and older – men on the island. Even when they had time off at the weekend the fishermen had to leave the boats at Burra and make their way home in their *fourerns*, weather permitting.

"I mind wan night … a few year before da War, on da 27th o February. An dey wir nobody dat ivver lookit for dem [expected them home from Burra] dat day. Dey rowed tree hours ta come past Symbister here [Houss Ness, half a mile] an dan dey towt dat hit wis too wet ta go onywye; ta try an win ashore onywye … an dan dey rowed anidder fowr hours [a further mile] afore dey got ta Havera. I mind a cousin o mine lookin in da door an he says … 'Welcome'. [laughing] Dey wir noboady ivver lookin. On a half-bad nicht dey wid always be on da go, lookin ta see if da boat …on yon night dey didna hae nae hoop o her comin at all."
John

SIX

A SHÖRMAL HAIRST

Besides seaweed for the *rigs*, there were other valuable commodities to be gleaned from the shore, such as flotsam and jetsam, and the occasional wreck.

Annie Deyell recalled the day a passing ship lost much of her deck cargo of timber, which came ashore in quantity on the beach at Hame Ham and how everyone, children and old folk too, helped stack it up well above the tide line. On occasion, when large baulks of timber came ashore, they were sawed up into planks at a sawpit, which may have been between convenient rocks on the beach of Hame Ham.[30] For this they used a two–man, long–bladed saw, one man above and one below, as happened all over Shetland. Such work required great skill to achieve slim, even planks for lining internal walls or making furniture.

So, a regular activity, when more pressing work was not required, was walking the cliffs to look for driftwood, particularly hardwood, and any other pieces of timber, or rope, or whatever might be turned to a useful purpose. Once, when the young John Williamson (1907) was out walking the cliffs with his brother the ground collapsed beneath him and he fell headlong with all the debris of earth and rock into the sea. Incredibly he survived to tell the tale. In recounting the event, to one person he said he did not tell his parents immediately as he knew he would have got a row for taking such risks; however, to others[31] he said that it was misty at the time and that his brother thought he was gone for good and that he ran home to get help. When they returned and John emerged hale and hearty above the cliffs, his brother thought he was a ghost! It is a tale that John delighted in telling and embellishing with further fantastic detail.

Wrecks were almost a common occurrence on the shores of Shetland in the days of sail. The earliest record of a wreck on Havera is of an

"The School Board provided only two tons of coal per session, but there was plenty of drift wood for the picking up. Once a ship lost her deck cargo of wood, and the whole of Hame Ham was packed solid. All except the very elderly women laid up wood for hours with the help of the bigger schoolchildren. Most of it was in bundles between two and eight feet long. We were all soaking from head to toe, but excitement kept us going ..... The Customs never came near us, and stacks and piles of wood lay rotting."
Annie Deyell.[32]

"I fell owre nearly da highest banks i da isle ... and when you look owre den you'll see dat hit was a miracle onyboady ivver cam oot o dere. Dat's whit ivery idder boady says; I dunna ken whit you micht say [laughing]. *Weel, hit was me an mi bridder wis traevellin doon da banks an yon was whit you wid caa 'rotten banks' and I said tae mi bridder 'watch oot' if he cam owre here an jöst wi dat, da whole thing gied ... jöst tons o hit ... an he was a bit farder back ... he didna go wi me, du kens. An I could see, du kens, iverythin dat was goin on sam as da stons on dis side ... you wid tink dat wi me no bein very heavy dat I wid a fa'an eftir da stons but I jöst seemed ta keep up da sam speed as da big stons, dat I could a laid mi haand on dem alangside. An dan, sin he gied doon tae da watter ... a big een jöst cam right alangside, du kens. I tink he was da biggest een o da bunch ... he kinda followed me ... keepin me company* [laughing]. *An dan I, du kens, for aa dat I was nivver laerned da sweemin lesson, I seemed ta hae nae budder o winnin ashore, but dey wir a lot a sea on, du knows, right i da very face o da cliff, an dat's da queerness bit o hit, fa'an owre da banks wisna; but dat wis gettin up, du sees. Even laandin, becaas da sea was heavy; heavy sea on."*
John Williamson.[33]

Waster Isle in the mist

Wrack wid

Wir gyos wis only fit for wrecks ta laand intil.
Hit's a ill wind dey say; an wrack wis gowld.
Wi siccan banks you took life ithin your haands

ta lay hit up ere you could bring hit haem. Eence
a tree—master creekst in, grundit, sails flaagin
an no a man aboard her. Haem Ham wis rampin

wi da hammerin; fae dan da place wis caa'd
Da Saa Pit. An eence, a boat lost a hael cargo:
her timber prammed dere, in below da banks

lik lumber dirlin doon da rapids. We vargit
till we hed hit stackit laek da paets, ivery een
o wis sokkit head ta fit, and spaegied.

Dat winter, paets bruckled i da stacks.
Dey wir roosters o fires; a new cradle, a kyist,
a dresser, a restin—shair an a boannie bed.

Whin we left Havera da hidmost time,
we rippit oot da plenishin, took da fine wid
wi wis. Hit med da best skeo—sheds in Burra.

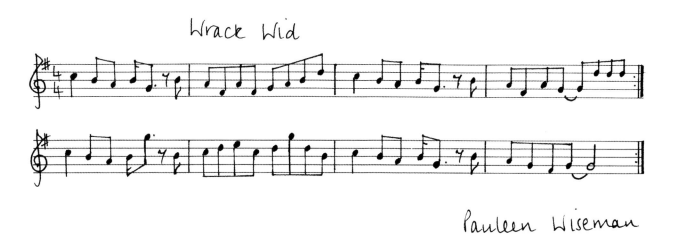

> *"On the 24th of said month [October 1773], an English vessel [the Grayhound] of 400 tons from Norway, load with saw stock, was driven by a storm of westerly wind on the rocks of Havra, when the whole crew perished in the night-time. About the same time also, a vessel [Batchelor] from Leith, with 260 emigrants for North Carolina, was by stress of weather put into Vela Sound in Walls."*
>
> **Rev John Mill**[34]

> *"… all went well until Saturday, when the wind began to increase in force, and the sea, which had been running pretty high, became more mountainous and the ship was badly buffeted. On Saturday night she had got well to the west of Foula, but at eleven o'clock the wind suddenly came away from the south-west with hurricane force, and the sea was lashed to fury. The vessel battled on for some time, but was threatened every moment to be engulfed. It was at this stage – shortly after midnight – that disaster overtook the vessel. One or two heavy seas broke on board and it was impossible in the darkness and hurricane to see any distance around. In fact the spray from the sea was going mast-high. Suddenly a huge wave made astern, and broke in over the vessel, clearing away deck fittings, smashing the hatches, and doing other damage. It was then realised that the first and second mates, and the boatswain were amissing. They had all been carried overboard by the wave and were never seen again in the darkness.'*
>
> **Shetland Times**[35]

unknown vessel with a cargo of tar going ashore on the northwest point of Havera around 1700. The next recorded wreck was the *Grayhound*, which went ashore, in 1773, before the island was settled with the families. Then there is a record of the wreck of a very similar ship called the *John and Mary* from Whitby in 1774[36], likewise laden with a cargo of saw stocks. There may well be confusion over the names of this vessel as the dates and cargo are so similar.

But the families were there in April 1903 when the disabled Norwegian three-masted barque, the *Lovise* of Drammen, was driven helplessly before a gale onto the rocks. She had left Newcastle with a cargo of coal bound for Brazil opting to take the north-about route.

The *Lovise* was driven before the wind off Fair Isle, the hatch covering was destroyed and she began to take in water and then the tide and wind took her north to the Shetland mainland. The Captain ordered the fore and main masts to be cut down to lighten the vessel, but she was no longer in control of her own destiny.[37]

The dramatic event, as the *Lovise* was driven onto Havera, was watched from Maywick by Robert Henderson and others. His son, Tom Henderson (1911–1981) wrote up an unpublished account from his father's description.[38] The events were also watched from the shores of Burra by, among

the many adults, a young boy named John Sinclair who, years later recorded what he had seen. It was a particularly emotional scene for him as his father was one of those who set off in *fourerns* from Burra to effect a rescue. This all happened less than a mile away but many times he lost sight of his father's boat as it fell into the trough of the huge waves. Fortunately, the *Lovise* drifted around to the more sheltered north side of Havera; there they launched their own small boat which could just carry three men and it managed to make the cliffbound shore. The story has it that the sheep were grazing on the seaweed on the beach and, when the dinghy with three seamen landed, the sheep took off up the narrow cliff path so leading the men onto the safety of the green. The rest of the crew made it off in a larger boat but they had only one oar.

It was Sunday on Havera and no one was out working or aware of the drama that was taking place less than a mile away. However, it is said that an old lady went out to move her cow and she met the three seamen. Thinking at first that they were Burra men she put her arms around two and said *'come awa in then'* and took them to the south end of the island and the houses. The Havera men then at once launched their own boats and made for the wreck. Along with the Burra men they took the seamen from their one-oared lifeboat and brought them safely to Nort Ham.

Apparently, after landing, one of the survivors took off at a run and was chased by a Havera man who thought he was demented and meant to throw himself off the cliff.[40] However, it turned out he was just trying to get dry! The only seaman lost at Havera was the ship's carpenter who had dived into the water to try and swim ashore. His body was washed ashore at Minn on Burra the next day and, following tradition, was buried there, his grave marked by a stone. In 1996, 93 years later, his great grandson came from Germany and tracked it down.[41]

There is an account of water running from the seamen's clothes beneath the door of one of the houses into which they were taken for shelter and warmth; and of a man of the house taking off his trousers and giving them to a shivering and soaking seaman who broke into tears at that act of instinctive humanity.[42] The ten men stayed on Havera overnight before beginning their long journey home the next day. In gratitude for saving their lives the Captain gave his gold ring inscribed with his name, Alberth, to Margaret Jamieson (1880), in whose family hands it still resides. In addition there is a silver watch held by one of the families, which is said to have come from one of the crew.

The following month a letter arrived from one of the survivors, written by G Christoffersen, editor of the Svelviksposten, Svelvik, Norway. It was dated 20th April 1903 and addressed to John Williamson, Havera Isle, Shetland. In it, Anton Admundsen of the wrecked barque *Lovise* of Drammen conveyed his thanks for the kindness shown to them.

Other material reminders of the wreck of the *Lovise* are large pieces of iron from the ship on the beach at North Ham, still in use, for tying up boats, more than one hundred years later.

"One of my chores was to look after the sheep and lambs. This day was especially bad: a strong westerly gale was blowing and a very heavy sea was running … I accidentally happened to look in a westerly direction. I think that my heart stopped temporarily. I had to convince myself that I was actually seeing in reality what was before my eyes – a large sailing ship with her sails torn, drifting towards the isle of Havera … When I again saw the ship she was riding at anchor a short distance off the rocks. [but] Her anchorage broke due to the pressure of the wind and the force of the heavy seas … she was carried broadside by a terrific wave on to a rock ledge … [she] fell back and drifted around the rocks … commencing to settle lower in the water and finally sank below the waves … some of the women folks cried, some screamed, one fainted."
John C Sinclair[39]

D25/120

„Svelviksposten"'s Expedition.

Svelvik den April 30th 1903

Mr John Williamson
Havera Isle

Dear Sir.

Mr. Anton Amundsen, Steward
on the wrecked Bark "Louise" of Drammen,
wishes to express to you and your family
his sincere thanks for the great kindness
and help you showed towards him
and his son Henry during their
stay with you. He says, he will not
soon forget your many kind acts, and
~~trust~~ that the blessing of God may follow
you.

He also wishes me to say that
~~that~~ they got home safely nine days
after leaving your place, and is now
about to leave for the Baltic.

2

„Svelviksposten"'s Expedition.

Svelvik den _____ 190

You will also, Sir, please accept
my thanks for what you in this case
have done for my countryman and
a sailor in distress.

Yours very sincerely
C. M. Christoffersen
Editor of the „Svelviksposten".

Letter of thanks[43]

The unknown ship

There is a Havera story of an open boat being seen offshore, the occupants of which were clearly in distress and unable to row; all the survivors of a ship that had foundered. A Havera boat went off to tow it in, finding within it four seamen dead, including the Captain, and five barely alive, one of whom subsequently died once ashore. Such was the respect of the seamen for their Captain that, along with the others, they buried him on Havera complete with his untouched money purse … perhaps they owed him their lives. And so the Captain lies with his coins in his grave on Havera to this day. The four surviving seamen recovered and made their way to the mainland and on to Scotland. En route south, while crossing the Tay, the story goes, either the ferry capzised or the Tay Bridge collapsed – which would make it 1879 – and they were all drowned!

There may be some confusion about the date of this wreck as John Williamson (on tape) recalls another wreck in 1879. The *Alpha*, a brand new fishing boat which was on its way from Lerwick, around the south end of the Shetland mainland to Burra (with a Burra crew), went down in bad weather. A hatch from the boat came ashore on Havera and was used in the kiln where it was discovered when the kiln was repaired in 1919. It is said that someone from the Burra area had been at Lerwick and refused an offer of a trip home on the *Alpha*. He had recalled that before the boat sailed, the men had complained that the new ropes were sticking in the blocks. It is surmised that in the poor weather they had been unable to loose the sheets and quickly trim the sails when caught by the wind and had capsized.

But more than one seaman's body is buried on Havera. There is the story of a naked body being washed ashore and buried, and the remains of another, though Jessie Williamson (1903) was convinced it was the same body, was unearthed in 1974 by John Robert Jamieson (1915) when a sheep was being buried. In the first story, an old woman wrapped up the body in a good blanket that she could ill–afford to lose. That night she dreamed that she was to receive a reward for her kindness and sacrifice. The next day she went down to where the body had come ashore and found a parcel. Inside was some Shetland hosiery. She took this to Lerwick and sold the knitwear for cash. It was then recognised as having been previously sold to a Norwegian seaman. Somehow the parcel had become lost overboard from his ship on the west side and she had found it … and been rewarded!

"On one side of the gjo [Nort Ham], on the grassy slope above the rocky cliffs, there was a patch of brilliant green grass. This was the last resting place of a shipwrecked crew. There being no graveyard on the island, and the weather too stormy for interment elsewhere, they had been buried where they came ashore."
Annie Deyell

Havera monster

No island story is complete without a monster. It is said that, many years ago, fishermen rowing out from Havera to the *haaf* were followed by some sort of animal, the like of which they had not seen before and that this happened on two successive days. Being afraid that they might be capsized they sought the advice of the laird. He told them to take a buoy – which in those days consisted of the blown–up stomach of an ox – and, when there was a fresh north wind, throw it towards the whale which, hopefully, would follow it. They took the buoy and, when once again they met the monster, they did as instructed. Just as the laird had predicted, the monster followed the drifting buoy over the horizon and was seen no more.

"One day as they left the Isle and were rowing out to sea they saw a large dark object in the distance; after a few minutes they realised it was swimming towards them at great speed and making a big disturbance in the water. When it was almost alongside it dived below the boat nearly upsetting them in its wake, and they were very frightened and pulled away as hard as they could row back to Havera. It kept following them breaking the surface and diving below the boat all the way till they reached the shelter of the Isle … None of the fishermen had ever seen a creature like this before; they had seen whales, sharks and neesiks many a time, but this one was greenish/grey colour and seemed to be covered in scales on the upper part of the body, and much larger than a whale."
Alex Mouat.[44]

SEVEN

HIGH DAYS AN HELLI-DAYS

"Dey aalways tried ta come in eence ivery week, an dey did come ivery week. Hit wis a owld man fae Papil. His name was Jeemie Kendall Smith. An he cam wi some very coorse days."
Jessie

The Postman at Nort Ham

Originally there were five small crofts on Havera which subsequently became four. Only the firstborn son (or daughter, if there were no sons) could inherit. So, in the hundred and fifty years that the families were on Havera there was a frequent exodus of young people, many of whom went to nearby Burra or the Shetland mainland while others emigrated. Of the seven surviving children of Walter (1824) and Margaret (1826) Williamson, two sons at least emigrated to New Zealand and Canada respectively; one daughter married a Burra man and settled there; while an unmarried brother and sister also settled together on Burra. Another branch of the families in which emigration took place was the family of George (1820) and Mary (1822) Jamieson: three of their eight sons went to the USA.

The young men of Havera regularly made trips outwith the island, for example, to Scalloway with fish, to Maywick with grain and to Burra for supplies. They had opportunities to meet young women and more than one Havera lad married a Burra lass. But for their sisters, the opportunities to meet eligible young men were far fewer, at least until the opportunity came to go to the herring gutting at the end of the 19th century and beginning of the 20th century.

But Havera was not so isolated that they did not get a regular visit from the postman, once a week. At the turn of the century the incumbent was James Kendall Smith, an old man, in his seventies, who came from Papil in all weathers. He would stand at a certain spot at the top of the hill above the beach at Hame Ham to hand out the letters. Everyone came out of their houses to get them.

A series of postcards to Ann Jean Jamieson (1878) from her sister Margaret (1880) – known as Meggie – and from friends, between 1906 and 1922 indicate that Ann Jean worked at the herring in Scalloway, Lerwick, Sandwick and in England in the summer and autumn months. A postcard (summer, circa 1918) from Margaret to Ann Jean, who was then working at Brooniestaing, Sandwick, illustrates the physical challenges of getting to work after a weekend at home and the eagerness of Margaret herself to get to Scalloway. It seems that Ann Jean had been dropped at Maywick and then made her way the four or five miles (7–8 km) over the open hill back to work. *"Dear sister. Foo wan doo across the hill the streen? We are going to Scalloway today and Jackie [Jacobina Ann Laurenson 1881] is going to Burra and I wis doo wid been hame. Dey [their uncle, James Jamieson 1847] is coming to Scalloway we wis so we will likkly win hame if ever we win dere for we are waiting for a shower to clear up but it seems to be gathering on."*[45]

Currans for da cats

Sees du dis postcard, Meggie,
da first du ivver sent me, dat time
I gud ta Sandwick tae da guttin:
Mitchell's wis hit; or maybe Hakro's?
I ken at I wis tinkin lang for Havera,
an for da helly whin I'd win haem
ta gie you aa a haand. Whitna stravaig
back owre da hill fae Maywick.
Mind foo we ösed a meet up sometimes
at da paets, apön a boannie nicht;
I wid traik back tae da station, dug—tired;
watch you raise da sail for haem.
I could a gret.

An sees du dis een – a dose o smoorikins
apön him, but nae name! *'Hoping to see you
very soon my dear'*; postit in Scallowa.
A'm firyatten noo! My, whit time does!

Whit funs we hed in Lerrick:
da huts wis lichtsome an wis aye singin.
Even whan we hed ta wirk inta da hömin,
fingers tiftin, we still hed wis a spree.
Man, we wir tyoch, bendin owre da farlins
an da barrels, liftin creels an kerryin.
We wir nivver dön at Woods. Yun's Annie's card
fae Lerrick: still wirkin trowe September;
'twartree currans for da cats at Christmas!'
Shö aye said dat whan dey wir plenty herrin.

Du says du's missin me in dis een, an at
you're aa tattie hale! Du shurly wrat me
ivery time du gud ta Scallawa.   Bliss dee!
Hit wis da fine ta gyet da news fae haem.

An Isie's card: we wir baith sweet on
da sam boy, I mind. My Faader,
dat een's fae Willie Manson i da wartime!
Sent fae Glasgow. Wid you believe hit?
A fine laad he wis, but whittan bruck he wrat!
An dy een – wi richt news – sledgin da paets an
wir boys awa. Du soonds horrid trang wi wark.

Du didna lik whan I gud sooth ta Yarmooth.
Nae doot hit med da hairst seem lang an haevy.
Dat wis da days, jewel! Penga i wir pooches,
an shops ta spend hit in.

Kens du, I still draem aboot da guttin: hear
da rummel o barrels; an da Bressa Soond
prammed foo o drifters, bizzin laek bluebottles.
Lass, I wiss at dey hed löt dee come an aa.
Du wid a loved hit. But dey couldna spare
wis baith, I warn. I doot I wis da lucky wan.

(Gutters were paid 'piece—work', i.e. per barrel, so a long season meant higher wages. The reference to 'currants' in the correspondence
is most probably linked to the promise of some treats, especially fruit, for the family – even the cats – at Christmas time.)

Naani

i.m. Agnes Christie, 1858 – 1945

Naani nearly aye baed wi her sister's faemly.
Dey'd come fae Symbister, across da voe.
Shö barely gud ta scöl, jöst twartree weeks,

but yet could read an write. Ee day, six faemlies
left her wi aa da bairns o Havera an set der sail
ta Maywick tae da paets. Dat wis a day o him

for shö wis only eicht. Maybe shö tocht on
tedderin da peerie tings ta keep dem aff da banks?
Nae man ta better her, shö jöst baed on, browt up

faemly eftir faemly, but nane shö could ivver caa
her ain. Shö raised a hoose o fishermen. Eence,
whan gyettin aald, an aksed ta luik ta peerie Hansi,

whan hit cam time ta gie him back, couldna bear
ta pairt wi him, her virmishin still sair. His fock
tocht ill apön her; left him dere till shö wis

aff da isle dan took him haem. Naani loved bairns.
Wha dusna wiss ta hadd der ain, ta see dem growe?
But, dat shö wis loved bi mony, der little doot o dat.

Sadly neither Ann Jean nor her younger sister married, but the many postcards from Meggie suggest not just a measure of envy of the opportunity for adventure which she never experienced, but also hints at romantic encounters.

As well as fishermen lodgers there were also female domestic servants who were often relatives, or who became relatives. In 1861, in David Williamson's (1800) household, there was a 12 year old servant girl from Burra called Barbara Christie (1847). Perhaps by chance her cousin, Mary Christie (1848) visited Havera for in 1868 she married David Williamson (1842), son of David (1800). Mary then brought Agnes (1858) one of her younger sisters as a servant into their household. When Agnes, known as Naani, was just 8 years old she was left to look after all the Havera children younger than herself when the adults went off to Deepdale to the peats. She only ever had six weeks of schooling but could read and write. Naani stayed with the Williamsons throughout their married life. She was so fond of children that she went on, when she was 68, to bring up some of the next generation, Walter's (1883) children. Once when she was asked to look after Hansi (Hance Williamson 1905), Walter's nephew, son of his brother David (1871), she was not keen to give him back and his parents had to wait until she was off the island before they could retrieve him!

There was no church or chapel on Havera and the islanders went to Papil on Burra if they wished to attend a service or be married in church. They did not attend regularly but sometimes on a Sunday, when they did no hard work, they would simply dress up and sit quietly in a sheltered spot on the island and maybe sing a hymn or two. No islander was buried on Havera; anyone who died on the island was taken by boat and buried at the Papil graveyard. The only souls buried on Havera are those who were already dead when they arrived.

Happy group c1918

"We did jöst naethin [on a Sunday]; waakit roond da hill, a lock o wis tagidder … nae hoosewark… jöst a oardinary day … Da kye hed ta gien oot; dey hed ta be fed … You didna need ta kerry onythin on your back. You didna hae to go for no paets. Dat hed ta be taen in a Setterday. Watter hed ta be taen in a Setterday an, if you were fair stuck, you could go for a pel … hit wis [normally] kyerried in kegs fae da hill on your back …

Mam took wis ivery [Sunday] moarnin, me an Bob an Joahnie … we hed ta sit dere wi her afore two chapters [of the Bible] wis read, verse aboot wi her, so we kent we didna win ootside afore dan."
Jessie

High days an helli—days

Apön a simmer Sunday, if hit wis fair,
we'd rig wis up, daander tae da taatie höls,
salist for a meenit, maybe sing a hymn.

We'd luik doon apö wir haems, da yard,
wir rigs aa green, baess oot apö da hill.
Da sun wid glanse across ta Deebdaal,

an for a peerie little, we'd tak wir paes.
Nae makkin, nae dellin apö da Sabbath
an if da coo wis ridin, shö wid hae ta wait –

wis dreedin da wrastle ta gyet her tae da bull:
faels apö da tilfers, rowin her ta Maywick –
On high days an helli—days we'd sail ta Papil,

stiff collars studded in anunder oilskins, shön
for communion, flankers for da boat. Sometimes
dey wir a bairn ta christen, sometimes a coffin.

Pauleen Wiseman

Childhood and School

Treats for the children were simple and they made their own toys. As Jessie said: *"Mi bridder Bob … he med craedles oot o runts o kale … wi widden rockers … we pat wir dukkies in dem…med oot o bits o cloot, rowed up an rowed up …an dan we cled dem."* At Christmas some played the fiddle as Gideon recalled: *"I mind whan Christmas cam, dan dey wir yon owld man … he aalways got da music goin. Dey hed music, yon Jamiesons* [James Jamieson 1847]; *dey wir aa göd at playin da fiddle. Took little ta please wis."* And maybe they had some fruit as Jessie remembered: *"We herdly ivver saa lof* [loaf] *… an for fancies, weel, we saa a bit o cake at Christmas; a orange an aipple at Christmas. Nivver saa a orange or aipple trowe da week. Naeboady ivver saa dem …"*

But children were expected to play their part in the daily and seasonal round of adult tasks. For fetching peats from the peat stacks at Nort Ham each child, according to age, had an appropriate size of *kishie* to help and at a very young age they were given the responsibility of looking after those younger than themselves, so that older children and adults could get on with the work.

When Jessie, as a young girl, looked after children around the houses, adjacent to the cliffs, she tethered some for their own safety. *"Yae, we did. Some o dem could keep hit on an some wid not. Dey wir jöt mad!* [laughs] *… You jöst took a piece o tow an tied hit tae da door; jöst around da door. When dey wan tae da end o hit dey wir jöst rampin!"* Children started adult work at a young age. Jessie recalled that at nine; *"I wis hurlin a borrow dan, peerie borros dey med tae me and mi bridder … ta hurl da muck in."* Before school she churned milk while the boys might be in the barn threshing oats or bere. The precious grain was also winnowed by the adults using a flail, outside on a day when light wind would blow away the chaff. Thereafter it was dried in the communal kiln.

James (Dey) Jamieson (1847) and his wife Barbara (Baaby) Ann (1849)

Jessie Jamieson (1903) and her siblings with May Jane (1914) on her knee

"Weel, I mind whin I was … weel I could not a bön nine – an I aye luik at da young eens o nine noo – wir owld graand-uncle's fock …dey wir aa oot dellin … laek … hit was aa oppen fires, wi crooks hingin da kyettle on – a big iron kyettle – dey wid hing da kyettle up on da crook, an I wid come haem fae da scöl comin ta fowr o'clock, an I wid go in dere an wid wash up aa der dishes … an set dem on da table an dry dem an set dem up, dan fill dis kyettle again an hing hit apö da crook; an set da fire as best I could wi paets … an dan I'd go an help mi graandmidder –Mam – an mak ready wir tae … Shö [my mother] wisna very keen on da inside wark … shö maa'd girse an shö did iverythin. I hed da töl o da young eens … dey pat me doon apö da ayre wi aa da young eens o da Isle. … I nivver seemed ta tink I ivver wis a bairn."
Jessie

1

2   28

NAME	ADDRESS	ADM. NO.	BIRTH			AGE		ADMISS.			DIVISION	CLASS	FIXED DATE (Art. 29)		Atts. Brot. Ford
			D.	M.	Y.	MID YR.	END YR.	D.	M.	Y.			M.	Y.	
John Williamson	Havera Isle.	6	6	11	07			6	5	13		VI			298
Thomas Williamson	"	7	31	8	10			1	6	16		IV			402
Gideon Williamson	"	9	28	5	12			4	6	14		III			402
John R. Jamieson	"	12	18	4	15			23	8	20		I			340
Mary A. Jamieson	"	8	24	8	11			4	6	14		III			412
May J. Williamson	"	11	8	9	14			1	4	20		I			401

Week ending Sept. 2nd — Attendances

M.	T.	W.	T.	F.	3 TO 7	7 TO 10	OVER 10	SUPP.	TO DATE
x	x	x	x	x				6	6
x	x	x	x	x		10	10		10
x	x	x	x	x					10
x	x	x	x	x	10				10
x	x	x	x	x	10		10		10
x	x	x	x	x	10				10

Week ending Sept. 9th — Attendances

M.	T.	W.	T.	F.	3 TO 7	7 TO 10	OVER 10	SUPP.	TO DATE
x	x	x	x	x			10		16
x	x	x	x	x		10			20
x	x	x	x	x					20
x	x	x	x	x	10				20
x	x	x	x	x			10		20
x	x	x	x	x	10				20

ATTENDANCES SINCE ADMISSION

ACTUAL		POSSIBLE	
BROT. FORW.	TO CARRY FORW.	BROT. FORW.	TO CARRY FORW.

PRESENT {M. / A.

AFTER CANCELLING {M. / A.

SCHOOL OPEN

ROLL

| 6 | 6 | 6 | 5 | 5 | 20 | 10 | 20 | | 56 |
| 6 | 6 | 6 | 5 | 5 | | | | | |

TOTAL 56 AVERAGE 5·6

MORN.	AFT.	TOTAL
5	5	10

LEFT	ADM.	ROLL
—	—	6

ATT. TO DATE 56

| 6 | 6 | 6 | 6 | | 20 | 10 | 20 | 10 | |
| 6 | 6 | 6 | 6 | | | | | | |

TOTAL 60 AVERAGE 6

MORN.	AFT.	TOTAL
5	5	10

LEFT	ADM.	ROLL
—	—	6

ATT. TO DATE 116

Havera side-school Attendance Register, year ending 31st July 1922[46], courtesy of Shetland Museum and Archives

After education became compulsory in 1872 all the children attended school and they did not get off to help with the harvest or other seasonal work; education was taken very seriously. But there is an anecdote of one little boy who preferred to go off fishing and only attended school *"on days hit's no aff wadder"*!

The original school building, set on its own in the middle of the island, away from the township, was very small, about 16 feet by 12 feet (5 x 4 m). It was most probably thatched, with skylights as the only source of light. It may seem a strange place for it to be, such a long way from the houses. However, Gideon Williamson said *"… a fellow stayed here a long while ago"* and that when he left, the building became the school. Gideon is probably referring to the 19th century. The building may even have been part of a farm steading prior to the late 18th century. The school was what was called a 'side−school'. These usually occurred on small islands and the teachers were uncertificated ('pupil teachers') and paid low salaries.[47]

This old school building was used right up to around 1907 to the time Gideon Williamson (1869) took his family to Burra, presumably because he was away at the fishing all week and it was so much easier to get home to them without having to try and make the journey to Havera. They had been living in an extension to his parents' house in the township and this extension then became the new school. Only a decade before the last inhabitants left Havera there were still 20 children at the school.

Teachers were mostly young women such as Annie Deyell (née Goudie) from Bigton, who came and stayed on the island in 1916. Another was 'Chicago' Kate − so−called after emigrating and living in that American city for many years before returning to Shetland in her old age − alias Catherine Jamieson (1900) who was related to both Jamieson and

Gideon Williamson's (1869) house (far end) that became the new school

"We hed a kirn … ya …we did dat. I aye kirned dere … I hed ta kirn i da moarnin afore I gud tae da scöl. [Some boys] hed ta go ida barn an tresh da coarn. Wi a flail. Aalder fock took hit i da yerd, wi a kinda breezy day. Dey hed whit dey caa'd a flakki … Yes, sae da chaff aa gud fleein awa an da coarn wis left."
Jessie

Scöl

Some o wis Havera fock nivver hed a scölin
for dey wir nae end o wark for bairns' haands.
When we got a teacher, dat wis lichtsome for

dey baed wi wis, a week for ivery bairn. Dey'd
nae place ta caa der ain an, if dey got a bed,
dan dey wir lucky. Classes wis ben da hoose

for da but end wis a scutter wi da day's wark
an peerie tings nyiggin at da door, wantin in.
Whan Gideon left da isle we got his single–end

for a scöl–room. Wir fock tocht wis weel aff
for dey wir hed a mintie scöl wi naethin
but a skylicht trowe da taek, awa oot owre

near Sinclair's Stofa. We likkit helpin shiv
da muckle desks in place ta start da day. I mind
a table an a kyist. I tink dey wir a closet wi a bed.

We aa hed jobs ta help; a flör ta sweep, an,
i da winter, lamps ta trim an fill; a fire ta keep.
On simmer days, if hit wis fair, some boys gud

tae da haaf. Fae da scöl window we could scrime
Haem Ham, da colours shiftin wi da wind; could
barely wait for denner–time ta scale da banks,

strip aff an hae a dip. We'd bring back maa's eggs
for da teacher, partans or some whelks. Dey wir
books in ivery haem. Nane o wis whet laernin.

First class at school c1910; James Jamieson (1905), Jessie Williamson (1903), Jacobina Jamieson (1903) and Robert Williamson (1905)

"I tink we wid nivver a dön onythin at da scöl oota place, du kens … we widna a said ony cheek whit dey dö noo-a-days tae da teacher … I dunna tink we wid ivver a dön dat."
Gideon

"When school was over I swept the floor, moved the two big desks against the wall, and there was my living room. I had a table and a chair, my kist of course, a wooden biscuit box with a lid for groceries, and another standing on its end with a shelf in the middle. The latter made a little cupboard, the lid forming a door with leather hinges and a wave to shut it against mice. Here I kept my few dishes and my bread and marge. Bedding came from home, but the table and chair belonged to the place, as did a couple of paraffin lamps. Everyone used paraffin lamps in their houses, but still had collies [fish oil lamps] in their byres. There was nothing else I really required, and I would not have exchanged my lot with royalty."
Annie Deyell[48]

Boys at the beach c1918

> "… *nivver* [taught about] *Shetland; hit wis clean oot o hit. We nivver heard aboot hit.* [But] *we knew a graet lock aboot da outside wirld for dey wir dat mony paepers taen, for iveryboady wis a reader; dey wir most aafil readers.*
>
> *Da hale isle read.* [Her father encouraged them to read, but said] *Oh, göd books – don't read dat noavels! Dey wir nothin athin dat – pits nothin athin da head but nonsense. Don't ivver read dat! Read a richt book an dan do you sense."*
> **Jessie**

> "… *there was plenty of reading material on Havera, on a wide range of subjects. I am sure many a professor would have envied some of the folk there both for their libraries and their knowledge. It was there that I first made the acquaintance of the theory of evolution through Darwin's 'Origin of Species', and of many other subjects."*
> **Annie Deyell**[49]

Williamson Havera folk. Bright pupils often became pupil−teachers in these schools. In the 1891 and 1901 censuses Elizabeth Williamson (1875) was listed as a teacher and may have continued teaching for longer. Originally, the teachers – generally young women – stayed with the families, sharing a room with the pupils and moving from one house to another, getting a week's bed and board per child per term.[50] If there were three children attending school in one family then she would stay there three weeks. So Annie Deyell must have been well pleased when she moved into the new school.

In the new school there was a stove and the children sat three to a desk. To begin with they used a slate and pencil; later pen and ink. But when it moved into the extension in the township it also became the teacher's home and she had a bed in what was described as a 'closet' in the schoolroom.

The children were taught all the usual subjects but never about Shetland. But it was typical of Shetland of the time that they were all very well read.

Jessie's Reading book

EIGHT
DA HIDMOST YEARS

The beginning of the end came slowly, prompted largely at first by changes to the fishing. The 1881 fishing disaster when Walter Jamieson (1835) and his son, Walter (1863) were lost, was a reminder, if it was needed, of just how dangerous open–boat fishing was in Shetland. The events that day must have caused a lot of discussion on the island and perhaps a desire for larger, safer boats. Due to uncertain markets, there was also a decline in interest in winter haddock from Hay & Co, the main purchaser at Scalloway.[51]

It was a sign of just how successful the Havera fishermen were that in 1898, David (1871) and Gideon (1869) Williamson, their cousin John (1871) Williamson, and Alexander Pottinger of Burra Isle, became owners of the *Sea Bird*, a decked boat of 46 foot (15 m) keel from which they fished for white fish by lines and for herring by nets. This was a major development after one hundred years of open–boat fishing; a leap forward that was being taken by many other Shetland fishermen. However, even as recently as 1900 some – perhaps the older Havera men – were still fishing long line for cod and ling in the summer months, and haddocks in the winter, from their open boats.

The following year of 1901 there were four families recorded at the census, comprising a total of 25 adults and children; half the number of 1851. Ten of the men were still described as fishermen and most of the women as knitters. By 1908 they had sold the *Sea Bird* and bought the *Gowan*, a larger decked boat of 60 foot (20m) keel which was later renamed the *Guiding Light*. It was owned by David Williamson alone and crewed mainly by Havera men. Then they had the *William Gladstone* and the *Camperdown*, the latter belonging to the Jamieson family. For any small island community this was a major achievement but, ironically, it was their undoing.

Ten years later, in the 1911 census, there were

Davie Williamson (1842) and Elizabeth (Leebie) Williamson (1840)

5 households listed: David (1842) and Mary Williamson's (1848) household was down to seven; Robert Christie Williamson (1827) had died and his son John (1871) was now head of a household of nine; James Jamieson's (1847) household comprised three; James Jamieson (1841) had died and the household of seven was headed by his son Robert (1875); the latter's brother, Thomas (1872), also had a household of three. The total on the island on the day of the census was now 29. Perhaps significantly, two of the old hands had gone, Robert Williamson (1827) and cousin James Jamieson (1841) above.

These figures, however, conceal the fact that by now all the able–bodied men were fishing away from Havera in large decked boats which could not be kept at the island. Their catch of haddock might be landed at Scalloway but sometime they were landing herring in Lerwick and the men only returned home at the weekend when they could, at least when the weather was reasonable. This could not go on.

> *"Da men gied tae da simmer fishin* [herring] *an dan dey gied to Lowestoft* [mid September – late November]. *Dey didna geeng* [any longer] *ta nae lines* [traditional open–boat line fishing]*, less jöst a bit o a line … for da saat fysh or onythin tae demsels. An da boys an da owld men gied ta whit we caa 'da shuttin' … dat wis da handlin … an dey got haddocks, splendeed haddocks … for da saatin; an piltocks."*
> **Jessie**

1 ENUMERATION BOOK 1

Civil Parish and Parish Ward of	Ecclesiastical Parish or Quoad Sacra Parish of	School Board District of
Lerwick : Landward	Quarff	Lerwick

Parliamentary Constituency of: Orkney & Shetland

Municipal Burgh or Police Burgh of: Part in East Burra " Havera

No. of Schedule	ROAD, STREET, &c., and No. or NAME of HOUSE	Houses Inhabited	Rooms with one or more Windows	NAME and SURNAME of each Person	Number of Persons in House	RELATION to Head of Family	Age Males	Age Females	Gaelic or G. & E.	Marriage Condition	Duration of Marriage	Children born Alive	Children still Living	Personal Occupation	Industry or Service	Employer/Worker/Own Account	If Working at Home	BIRTHPLACE	Nationality
1	Havera Isle	1	3	David Williamson	7	Head	68			Mar				Crofter & Fisherman	20	Own Account	at Home	Havera Isle Shetland	
				Mary Williamson		Wife		63		Mar	43	6	5					Burra Isle Shetland	
				Walter do		Son	24			S				Fisherman	20	W		Havera Isle Shetland	
				Elizabeth do		Daur		35		S								do	
				Mary do		Daur		21		S								do	
				Agnes Christie		Serv		52		S				Domestic Servant				Burra Isle Shetland	
				Catherine Williamson		Sister-in-law		50		Mar	20	1	1					do	
2	do	1	3	John Williamson	9	Head	39			Mar				Crofter & Fisherman	20	Own Account		Havera Isle Shetland	
				Jessie do		Wife		31		Mar	8	4	4					Burra Isle - do	
				Jessie do		Daur		7						School				Havera Isle do	
				Robert do		Son	6							School				do	
				John do		Son	3											do	
				Thomas do		Son	under one mo.											do	
				May Webster do		Mother		76		W				Private Means	1			Burra Isle do	
				Ann Jane do		Sister		51		S				Knitter	40	Own Account	At Home	Havera Isle do	
				Gideon do		Nephew	25			S				Fisherman	20	Own Account		do	
3	do	1	4	James Jamieson	3	Head	63			Mar				Crofter	19	W		Sandwick Shetland	
				Barbara do		Wife		61		Mar	31	none						Havera Isle "	
				Jessie Smith		Aunt		91		S								do.	
4	do	1	4	Robert Jamieson	7	Head	35			Mar				Fisherman & Crofter	20	Own Acct		Burra Isle do	
				Jacobena do		Wife		29		Mar	6	2	2					Dunrossness do	
				Janet do		Mother		67		W				Private Means	1			Havera Isle do	
				James do		Son	5											do	
				Walter do		Son	4											do	
				Ann do		Sister		32		S				Knitter	40	Own Acct		do	
				Margaret		Sister		30		S				Knitter	40	do		do	
5	do	1	2	Thomas Jamieson	3	Head	35			Mar				Fisherman	20	W		Sandwick Shetland	
				Willimina do		Wife		38		Mar	4	1	1					Sandwick Do	
				Jacobena do		Daur		7						School				Burra Isle do	

Total of Houses 5 — Total Windowed Rooms 14 — Total Persons 29 — Total of Males 12 — Total of Females 17

1911 Census, courtesy of Scotlandspeople

"Da young fock began to go oot ta work: da boys aa gied an dan dey wir two owld men – da men wis aa i da War, da First World War – an dan dey wir two owld men – dey wir seventy – an dey did da sailin o da boats back an fore. Hit wisna very göd sea i winter; an dan dey cam at dey wirna able ... da boys couldna bide haem – oot o Scallawaa – da fock wis gyettin owlder, sae dey jöst aa left ... 1922."

Jessie

Gideon Williamson (1869), one of the co–owners of the first decked boat, the *Sea Bird*, had left the island with his family in 1907; when their house became the new school. When Mary (née Christie 1848), wife of David Williamson (1842), died in 1914, he too left, taking his sister–in–law and most of his remaining children. They took with them their household furnishings and all their belongings, settling first in Scalloway then Burra, leaving three remaining families. There were still eleven boats in use on Havera in 1913[52] and there would have been a reluctance for others to leave, though by 1914 it seems that the last of their distant neighbours on the Peerie Isles – Linga and Oxna – had left; leaving Havera as the last small Shetland island to hold a community. 1914 also brought the Great War and that took another four able–bodied Havera men into the Royal Navy for the next four years.

Barely six years later, in 1920, David's remaining son, Walter Williamson (1883), his wife Margaret (née Fraser 1886) and their three children left with all their belongings, once again first to Scalloway and then to Burra.

The following year, on the 8th December 1921, David's nephew, John Williamson (1871), his wife, Jessie (née Sinclair 1879), their eight children, their furniture and all their belongings and livestock were

Camperdown LK 1117[53], courtesy of Shetland Museum and Archives

also flitted in small boats from Havera to a croft at Symbister in East Burra. Among the children were Jessie (1903), John (1907) and Gideon (1912) – who made the recordings. A year later, in 1922, when Barbara (Baaby Ann, 1849) died, her widower, James (Dey) Jamieson (1847), left for Scalloway.

That left just thirteen people of two families The first was Robert Jamieson (1875), his mother Janet (1844), his wife Jacobina (née Laurenson 1881) and their five children; also his unmarried sisters, Ann Jean (1878) and Margaret (Meggie 1880), the former often away to the herring gutting as far as Gorleston in Norfolk.[54] The other was Thomas Jamieson (1872), his wife Williamina (1872) and their daughter. This last group remained on Havera but a year. In April 1923, they too packed up all their belongings and left the isle for Burra, leaving Havera uninhabited.

"Weel I tink hit wis, du sees ... you hed ta come ta Scallawa here for your stores, you wid say, an in ony bad weather, you know whit lik hit is here ... hit wis seeven mile ... on Burra you could walk ta da shop, du sees ... hit was unhaandy ... If onyboady maybe got badly ... if you'd gotten ill at ony time you wid hae tae a gone wi ... hit widna matter whit laek, should [it] be a storm, sees, hit micht a come a storm, you micht nivver a gotten oot o da isle, du sees. An dat wis tön inta consideration ... didna hae a motor boat. I believe if dey hed gotten a motor boat dey might a stayed, du sees ... everythin wis in a oppen boat an sailin, an dan sometimes you hed bad weather ... you could hardly row up wi yon severe gales, du sees, Hit wis aa hard wark."

Gideon

... an dat's Havera

Wir aa bön ta Havera: a place twined
wi wir ain peerie isles; a green embrace
cut aff fae da wirld, wi hits ain time,

a graet sky abön, a ocean froadin
at hit cöts. Da wirld awa oot dere
on a different scale. Feelin smaa, an

hüld in hits bosie, wi da isle we lö
tae da sea's haert—baet, hits rhythm,
hits wye o bein. Affen shö skiled

da horizon for him ta win haem safe
an soond, mak hit ta da gyo. Wha's
no sowt a noost in some Nort Ham?

An days o dellin an ripin tagidder,
o layin by for a lang winter. Maistlins
noo we can only draem o sharin.

An whan a stranger cam, dey wir
a bed an maet, a dram, a göd yarn.
An, if need be, a sheet for a yirdin.

c1920/1. Backrow; James (Dey) Jamieson (1847) first from left, Margaret Jamieson (1844) second from left, David Wiliamson (1842) third from left, Jessie Williamson (1903) fifth from left, John Williamson (1907) seventh; middle row: Jessie Williamson (née Sinclair 1879) third from left, the postman James Kendall Smith third from right, John Williamson (1871) second right (with a child on his knee): front row; Gideon Williamson (1912) third from left

Postscript

> *"Dey seemed ta say dat if dey had no a left at da time dat dey did leave ...dis engines wis comin on da go dan, an dan da telephones wis comin, you see ... an dey seemed ta tink dat dey widna a left if dey jöst hed a stuck oot a year or two longer, you ken. I mind someboady got a big box fae Scallowa an dis wid a been [would have been a box for an] engine ... smaa boat's engine, an a graanduncle o mine wrat right til America aboot dat engine."*
> **John**

In 1922, after they had left Havera, the brothers David (1871) and Walter Williamson (1883) and their cousins, John Williamson (1871) and Gideon Williamson (1885) bought the steam drifter, *Girl Lizzie* with which they fished for a number of years. It says much about the hard work, productivity and success of the Havera fishing men and their families over several generations that from enforced beginnings in open boats, they were able to move on to decked boats and from there accumulate the substantial funds to purchase such a state of the art steam fishing boat.

Nearly all the last inhabitants of Havera moved to Burra and Scalloway. After they left, Bruce of Symbister offered the four families who had the tenancies of the isle, the opportunity to buy it. At the going rate, as tenants, it would have been a bargain; however they declined. Around the middle of the 20th century, Barclay, a butcher from Sandwick bought the island, thinking he could raise sheep for his business. But, of course, the tenants had the grazing rights so his plans came to nothing. Perhaps roused by this turn of events, the tenants then bought the isle and today it is, appropriately, in the hands of four descendants of the original families.

Steam Drifter *Girl Lizzie* LK 175[55], courtesy of Shetland Museum and Archives

> *"Weel hit wis jöst da fock. An da kind o wark you did an dat things ... you missed aa dem. Iveryboady missed dat. Hit [Burra] wis different ... different life, Burra ... hit wis a easier life. Hit wisna sae lichtsome. No. Na, dey wir aa tagidder at Havera; iveryboady wis mixin. You couldna geeng oot o da Isle less aa haands gied ... Ivery hoose hed ta ken whit da next hoose wis döin. Hit wis laek wan hoose ... hit wisna laek iveryboady didna hae a hoose tae demsels ... hit wis wan hoose."*
> **Jessie**

Still neebirs

Maistlins der at Papil noo, da Havera fock,
borne nort owre da Quairk; a hidmost time
bi Houss Ness, da Peerie Holm o Clett.

Maybe a neebir's boat tön for da börial,
da oars' rhythm fornenst tide, or rinkel
o riggin. A dark runk, lug sail dippin:

a dookin, a hidmost baptism; haddin tagidder
i da face o brevity, da dunts o laevin; an
mindin on peerie tings at nivver med hit.

Dan liftit wi care, shoodered bi faemly
an freends dat hard green step; lowered
peerie–wyes, da coards lik humlibaands,

steadyin progress trowe da traugh, a text
laid kindly owre dem – o a new Jerusalem
a new Havera – hüld i da fastibaand o aert.

Family Trees
Extended family chart for Walter Williamson

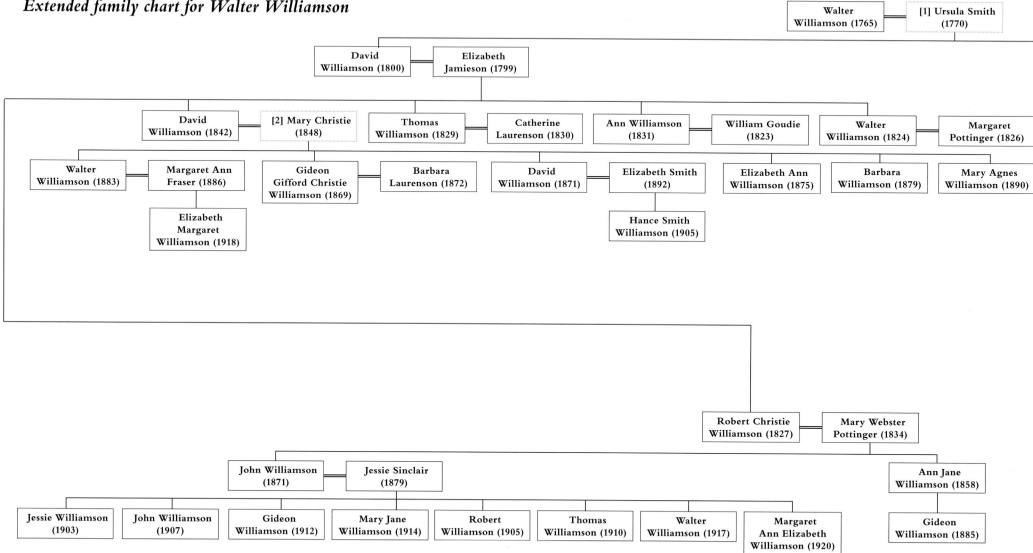

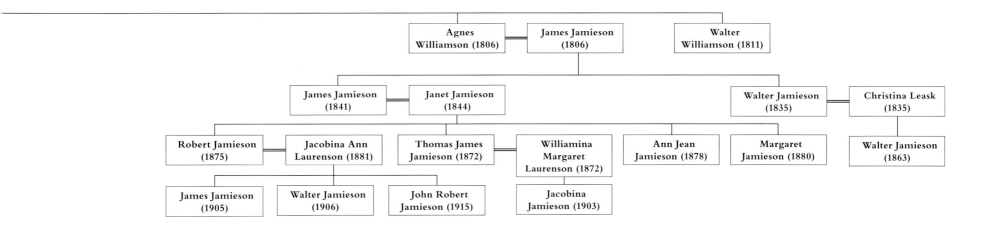

Agnes Williamson (1806) — James Jamieson (1806) — Walter Williamson (1811)

James Jamieson (1841) — Janet Jamieson (1844)

Walter Jamieson (1835) — Christina Leask (1835)

Robert Jamieson (1875) — Jacobina Ann Laurenson (1881)

Thomas James Jamieson (1872) — Williamina Margaret Laurenson (1872)

Ann Jean Jamieson (1878)

Margaret Jamieson (1880)

Walter Jamieson (1863)

James Jamieson (1905)

Walter Jamieson (1906)

John Robert Jamieson (1915)

Jacobina Jamieson (1903)

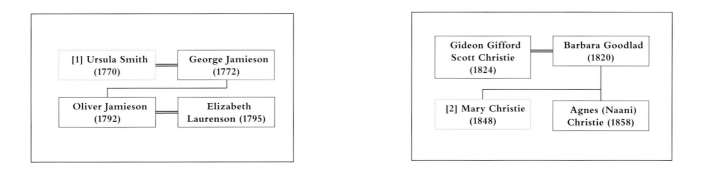

[1] Ursula Smith (1770) — George Jamieson (1772)

Oliver Jamieson (1792) — Elizabeth Laurenson (1795)

Gideon Gifford Scott Christie (1824) — Barbara Goodlad (1820)

[2] Mary Christie (1848)

Agnes (Naani) Christie (1858)

Family Trees
Extended family chart for George Jamieson

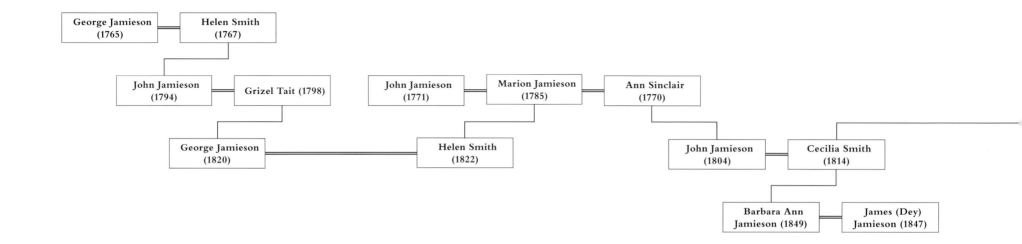

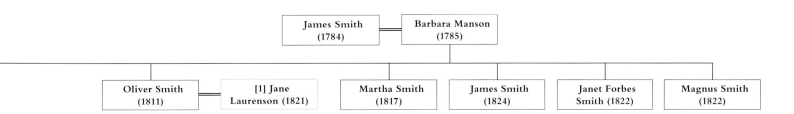

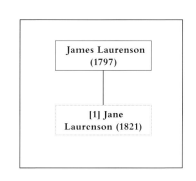

Glossary

aafil	very, thorough
aawye	everywhere
abön	above
aer	small quantity
aert	earth
aert—bark	tormentil (root)
affa	off
affen	often
airrands	shopping messages
antrin	occasional
anunder	underneath
argie—bargie	quarrel, dispute
baandless	loose (derogatory)
baed	stayed, lived
baess	cattle
bafft	struggled (from noun)
bain	thick leather
banks	sea cliffs; peat cuttings
barmin	frothing, seething
bassel	struggle
beelt	built
ben da hoose	best room in cottage
birsed	squeezed
bismar	wooden weighing beam
blaand	sour whey
black fantin	famished
boo	bow of boat
borrow	barrow
bosie	bosom
bördly	robust, strong
böt	boot
brennastyooch	fine sea spray
brigdi	basking shark
briggisteyns	footpath of flat stones in front of house
broo	brow

brönnie	round, thick oatmeal scone
bruck	remnants, refuse
bruckled	broken, fragmented
brunt	burned
budder	bother
bulder	blunder along clumsily
bummeled	floundered
bush rope	bottom rope of a net
but	kitchen end of cottage
caa	drive sheep
claggy	sticky
cled	clad
cloorin	scratching with claws
clowe	clove
coarn	oats
coo	cow
coortin	courting
cöst	cast
cotts	petticoats
cöt	ankle
creekst	move painfully
crö	sheep—fold
crub	small dry—stone enclosure for cabbage plants
crump	crunch
curran	raisin, currant
dander	wander
daffik	small wooden bucket
datn	so very
dee	you (objective, familiar)
dell	dig
dilled	died down
dippilt	planted, using a dibble
dirlin	shaking, vibrating
doocot	dovecote
dookin	soaking

doot	doubt
dose	a large number
du	you (subject, familiar)
dukkie	doll
dunder	loud noise
dunt	heavy blow
ebb	foreshore
een	one; eyes
ert	(wind) direction
Faader	Father (God)
fael	sod or turf
faert	frightened
fantin	hungry
farlin	large troughs filled with herring for gutting
fastibaand	cross—beam under thwarts of boat, for strength
fekkit oot	looped out as for ropes
feth	mild oath
filskit	high—spirited, frisky
filt	filled
fire kyettle	cast—iron pot used in boats for holding cooking fire
firyatten	forgotten
fit	foot
flaagin	flapping loosely
flakki	straw mat over which oats were winnowed
flan	sudden squall
flankers	long sea—boats
flet	expressed anger
flit	move – especially to move house, or cattle to fresh grazing
flit—boat	boat used to transport loads from large vessel to shore
flooer	flour

flör	floor		gunwales with stem	luik ta	look after
fock	folk	hirdit	gathered crops	maa	seagull
foo	how; full	horrid	very (adding emphasis, generally	maet	food
fornenst	against		positive)	maistlins	almost, nearly, mostly
froad	foam, froth	höl	hole	makkin	knitting
funs	enjoyment	hömin	twilight	mallie	fulmar petrel
gansey	jumper	höved	heaved, threw	man	must
girnal	large meal−chest	humlibaands	loop of rope holding oar in place	meid	landmark for navigation
girse	grass	hüld	held	mid−room	section of sixern near mast for ballast
glansed	sparkled	janderin	in heat		or fish
gligg	hole in barn wall through which	jewel	term of endearment	mind	remember
	sheaves were passed	kabe	thowel−pin of a boat	mintie	tiny
gliv	glove	kavvel	extract the hook from the mouth of	mirackled	injured severely
glufft	frightened		a fish with a notched stick	mirknin	twilight
göd	good	kirknin	first attendance at church as married	mirry−begyit	illegitimate child
gret	wept		couple	mizzered	measured
gud	went	kirn	churn	muckit	applied dung
gyaain	going	kirsen	fit to eat or wear	naewye	nowhere
gyo	narrow, rocky sea cleft	kishie	cane or straw basket for the back	neebin	nodding with sleep
haaf	deep sea fishing	klined	spread, as butter	neebir	neighbour
haandless	clumsy, lacking practical skills	kye	cows	neebrid	neighbourhood
hadd	hold	kyempin	competing	neep	turnip
hael	whole	kyerried	carried	neesik	porpoise
haem	home	laad	boyfriend	neist	next
haepit	heaped	laek	like	niffin	smelling
hain	use sparingly	laem	crockery	njuggelsteyn	projecting stone in barn wall on
hairst	harvest	lib	castrate		which oats were threshed
halliget	wild, unrestrained	lichtsome	cheerful	noost	hollow or structure above beach for
hansel	inaugural gift	linn	piece of wood or whalebone laid on		safe housing of boat
hap	shawl		beach to facilitate moving a boat	nyiggin	tugging
heads ta traas	laid heads and feet alternating	lippenin	expecting	onkerry	carry−on, disturbance
heist	hoist, heave	lith	joint or segment of bone structure	owsin	baling out water
helly	week−end	longie	common guillemot	örmals	scraps, remainder
helly days	holy days (formerly feast days)	lö	listen intently	ösed	used
hidmost	final	lönabrak	surge of sea breaking on shore	ots	oats
hinny−spot	triangular piece of wood connecting	löt	let	paand	valance

paes	peace
partan	crab
peerie	small
peerie little	small quantity
peerie ting	little one, infant or child
peerie-wyes	gently
penga	money
piltock	mature coal-fish
plank	consolidate dispersed tenancy of arable land into one piece
planti-crub	small dry-stone enclosure for cabbage plants
poo	pull
pooch	pocket
pöl	pool
prammed	crammed, squeezed together
pyaa (no fit ta)	extremely exhausted
quaig	heifer
quilk	swallowing sound, gulp
raise	set up wet peats to dry
rampin	boiling fiercely
reesel	rummage (noisily)
reestit	smoke cured
rekk	reach
restin-shair	long wooden seat with back and arms
ribbeen	ribbon
ridin	in heat (cow)
rig	field; to dress
riggy	spine
rinkel	tinkling noise
ripin	digging up potatoes
roo	pluck wool off a sheep
roogit	heaped
rooster	strongly blazing fire
rooth	piece of wood added to gunwale to prevent chafing by oar
roup	auction sale
röf	roof
röv	rivet-like fastening of boat planks
rummel	collapse
runk	resounding rhythm
runnik	open drain from byre, usually to midden
saat	salt
sain	bless
salist	pause for a moment
scarf	cormorant
sclate	flat piece of wood fastened to oar to avoid chafing the rooth
scöl	school
scrime	observe with difficulty
sea-faerdy	sea-worthy
sel	seal
shaerd	sheared, cut grain
shappit	chopped
shiv	shove
shott	compartment near stern of sixern for holding fish
shön	soon; shoes
shörmal	high tide mark, water's edge
shrucken	shrunk
shuggar	sugar
shun	small loch
shut	cast line or net overboard
siccan	such
sidey-for-sidey	side by side
simmer blink	short gleam of sunshine
simmer dim	the period of long twilights in summer
sindered	separated
singilt	singled
sixern	six-oared wooden boat
skeetchin	splashing, spraying
skeo	structure, usually dry stone, or hut for wind-drying fish or meat
skiled	peered, looked with eyes shielded
sklent	tear
skroo	stack of oats
skurtit	gathered up and carried in arms
slidder	slither
smaa	small
smoorikin	kiss
smora	clover
sokkit	soaked
sopp	soap
sowt	sought
spaegied	having muscle pain from exertion
spang	leapt, bound
spleetin board	board at fishing station on which fish were split open
splore	turmoil, agitation
spree	jollification
starn	stern of boat
steekit	dense fog
steepel	fish piled crosswise on beach to dry
stivvened	became stiff with cold
stoor	strong breeze
stravaig	wander aimlessly
strug	toil
sware	evenly shared, neat, square
sweed	stung
swinklan	drunk
taatie höls	stores of potatoes in earth covered with turfs
taatit rugs	rugs of thick worsted yarn
taek	thatch
taes	feet on a brand iron (in this case)

taft	thwart, rowing seat
tagidder	together
teckin	tacking
tedder	tether
tidder	the other
tiftin	throbbing
tilfer	loose flooring—planks on bottom of boat
tinkin lang	missing place or person, feeling homesick
tirrick	arctic tern
tocht ill apön	felt sorry for
towes	long fishing lines, ropes
tö	too
töl	toil
tön	taken
tör	tore
traik	wander
trang	very busy
traugh	trough
trenkie	narrow passage or path
troo	through
trow	troll
trowe	through
tully	large open knife with wooden handle
tummelin	tumbling
tusk	fish of cod family
twartree	a few
tyoch	tough
uncan	strange, unfamiliar
varg	dirty, messy work
veggel	tethering stake in byre—wall
veggel—baand	rope attaching cow to stake in byre—wall
virmishin	longing

voar	spring planting time and associated work
voe	inlet of sea, generally long and narrow
waal	well
waar	seaweed; worse
waavelin	unbalanced, moving unsteadily
wadder	weather
warn	warrant
wastird	western part
wid	wood
wiss	wish
wheeft	whipped, swift movement
whern	quern
whet	ceased
whittan	what (emphasised)
wrack	sea—borne wood
wrastle	struggle
wrocht	worked
yirdin	burial
yoag	large mussel
yokk a hadd o	grasp firmly
yun	that (one)

References

1   Goodlad, Jessie SA 3/1/6/1 BBC Radio Shetland (1987)
2   Jakobsen, J (1936) The Place–names of Shetland. Nutt, London
3   Stewart, J (1987) Shetland Place–names. Shetland Library and Museum, Lerwick
4   Williamson, Gideon SA 3/1/29 BBC Radio Shetland (1988)
5   Leigh, H (1654) A Geographical Description of the Island of Burray. In Description of Ye Country of Zetland (1908). James Skinner & Co. Edinburgh
6   Hunter, R pers. comm.
7   Fenton, A (1978) The Northern isles: Orkney and Shetland. John Donald.
8   Leigh, H (1654)
9   G P S Peterson pers. comm., from John Williamson (1907)
10 Hunter, R pers. comm.
11 Leask, R pers. comm.
12 Deyell, A (1975) My Shetland. Thuleprint, Sandwick
13 SA D31/7/54
14 Deyell, A (1975)
15 Leask, J W (2002) Shetland Life. December.
16 Cowie, R (1874) Shetland Descriptive and Historical
17 Williamson, John SA 2/21/16/1 BBC Radio Shetland (1979)
18 ibid
19 Osler, A (1983) Open Boats of Shetland: South Mainland and Fair Isle. Maritime Monographs and Reports No 58. National Maritime Museum
20 Old Statistical Account (1793)
21 Goodlad, C A (1971) Shetland Fishing Saga. Shetland Times, Lerwick
22 Nicolson, J R (1982) Hay & Company. Hay & Company, Lerwick
23 Osler, A (1983)
24 Jamieson, R Jamieson Family History. Privately published. Hillprint, New Zealand
25 Nicolson, J R (1982) Hay & Company. Hay & Company, Lerwick
26 ibid
27 Jamieson, R Jamieson Family History.
28 Turnbull, Rev J (1851) Census
29 Leask, R (1976) We Tocht it wis da Laird, Shetland Folk Book 6
30 Hunter R pers. comm.
31 Jamieson, R pers. comm.
32 Deyell, A (1975) My Shetland
33 Williamson, John (1979)
34 Mill, Rev J (1889) The Diary of the Reverend John Mill 1704–1803.
35 Shetland Times 4th April 1903
36 Royal Commission of Ancient Monuments
37 Hansen, H L (2000) A shipwreck of 1903 recalled. Shetland Life March 2000
38 Henderson, T. The Norwegian Barque (unpublished), courtesy Ann Mouat
39 Sinclair, J C (1963) The Wreck of the Norwegian Barque "Louisa". The New Shetlander 143
40 Deyell, A (1975) My Shetland
41 Hansen, H L (2000)
42 Peterson, G P S pers. comm., from Johnnie Williamson (1872)
43 D25/120
44 Mowat, A (1986) The Havera Monster. The New Shetlander. 155
45 Postcards held by Adalene Fullerton
46 Scalloway Museum
47 Graham, J (1998) A Vehement Thirst after Knowledge, Shetland Times, Lerwick
48 Deyell, A (1975)
49 ibid
50 ibid
51 Nicolson, J R (1982) Hay and Company. Hay & Company, Lerwick
52 Osler A (1983)
53 Shetland Museum AF00025
54 Postcards courtesy Adalene Fullerton
55 Shetland Museum L00059